ROOT-TO-RISE

HOW TO LOVE LIFE

Workbook: Love Life by Design

CHANDRA LYNN, M.B.A.

GLOWLIVING.COM

ROOT-TO-RISE WORKBOOK: LOVE LIFE BY DESIGN

Published by Glow Living (Publishing Division of Glow Marketing LLC). All rights reserved.

This is a work of nonfiction. Some names, identifying details, and personal characteristics of individuals have been changed to protect their privacy.

Disclaimer: This book is intended for informational and personal development purposes only and is not a substitute for professional medical, psychological, or psychiatric advice, diagnosis, or treatment. The author is a certified life coach, not a licensed therapist. Readers are encouraged to seek support from licensed healthcare providers or mental health professionals for issues requiring clinical care.

ISBN (Paperback): 979-8-9986859-2-7

ISBN (eBook): 979-8-9986859-4-1

Cover design: Patrick Boyer, UrbanCowboy.net

Root-to-Rise® is a personal growth and development system comprised of a main guide book, —*Root-to-Rise: How to Love Life*—this companion workbook, journals, card decks, online courses, online communities, trainings and events, and more. Visit glowliving.com to see the complete collection.

Grateful acknowledgment is made to Chandra Lynn's supportive community, and Robbins Madanes Training for content related to human needs psychology and the Emotional Triad, as taught in their coach certification training.

Root-to-Rise®, Glow Living®, and Glow Marketing® are registered trademarks of Chandra Lynn, M.B.A.

For inquiries, contact:
chandra@glowliving.com
chandralynn.com
glowliving.com
glowmarketing.com

Printed in the United States of America
First Edition

ROOT-TO-RISE: HOW TO LOVE LIFE BOOK REVIEWS

"If you want a simple step-by-step guide for a fulfilled life, THIS is the book."
— **Dr. Deepak Chopra**

"Inspiring guidance for personal transformation, based on real-life work."
— **Kirkus Reviews**

"A wonderfully practical approach to nurturing balance and love in our everyday lives. A fantastic guide. Very highly recommended."
— **Readers' Favorite – 5-Star Seal**

"Customers find this book to be a powerful guide for personal growth, rich with valuable insights and tools that are practical for any stage of life. They appreciate its readability, with one customer noting it's accessible without being simplistic. The content receives positive feedback, with one review highlighting how it encourages readers to reconnect with their inner strength."
— **Amazon**

"Root-to-Rise encourages self-reflection and growth in the midst of life's messiness, offering practical exercises, helpful infographics, and grounded guidance."
—**The BookLife Prize**

"A soulful and practical guide for anyone seeking balance, emotional resilience, and a more fulfilling life."
— **Review Tales**

"A transformative self-help guide that empowers readers to navigate challenges, reconnect with purpose, and build a fulfilling life through a soulful, nature-based framework."
— **The Table Read Magazine**

→ If Root-to-Rise has made a difference in your life, please leave a review on Amazon, and share it with our community. Every review helps reach more people who may be struggling, searching for answers, or ready to create positive change in their lives. Thank you!

CONTENTS

A NOTE FROM CHANDRA LYNN 6

BEFORE YOU BEGIN 7

THE ROOT-TO-RISE FRAMEWORK 9

PHASE I: ROOTS 12

PART ONE • ROOTS 13

Chapter 4 • Root 1: Health – The Root of Vitality 14

Chapter 5 • Root 2: Family – The Root of Connection 17

Chapter 6 • Root 3: Relationships – The Root of Love 20

Chapter 7 • Root 4: Career – The Root of Purpose & Prosperity 23

Chapter 8 • Root 5: Friends – The Root of Support & Joy 26

Chapter 9 • Taproots 29

Chapter 10 • Roots Recap 32

PART TWO • NEEDS 33

Chapter 11 • Understanding Human Needs 34

Chapter 12 • Need 1: Security 35

Chapter 13 • Need 2: Variety 36

Chapter 14 • Need 3: Self 37

Chapter 15 • Need 4: Intimacy 38

Chapter 16 • Need 5: Growth 39

Chapter 17 • Need 6: Transcendence 40

Chapters 18–20 • Applying Human Needs & Needs Evaluation 41

PART THREE • CLEARING 54

Chapter 21 • Clearing the Way 55

Chapter 22 • Fear-based Resistance 56

Chapter 23 • Mental Clutter & Emotional Overload 58

Chapter 24 • Rewriting the Script 59

Chapter 25 • Hidden Emotional Traps 61

Chapter 26 • Foundation of Self-Respect 62

Chapter 27 • Clearing the Path 63

PHASE II: RESILIENCE 65

PART ONE • EMOTIONS 66

Chapter 28 • Navigating Emotions 67

Chapter 29 • Breaking Depressive Patterns 69

Chapter 30 • Energy Arrows 70

Chapter 31 • Happy Dance 73

Chapter 32 • Emotional Fitness for Relationships 75

Chapter 33 • Emotional Guidance System 76

PART TWO • ELEMENTS 77

Chapter 34 • Withstanding the Elements 78

Chapter 35 • Winds of Change 79

Chapter 36 • Storms of Life 81

Chapter 37 • Crashing Waves..82

Chapter 38 • Pressure Systems 84

Chapter 39 • Releasing to Rise 86

Chapter 40 • After the Storm 89

PHASE III: RISE 91

PART ONE • AUTHENTICITY 92

Chapter 41 • Connecting to Authenticity 93

Chapter 42 • Unveiling the Masks 94

Chapter 43 • Self-Confidence & Your Wild Side 95

Chapter 44 • Lightening Up 97

Chapter 45 • Standing True 99

Chapter 46 • Authenticity in Friendships 100

Chapter 47 • Intimacy & Vulnerability 101

Chapter 48 • Living Your Truth 104

PART TWO • BALANCE 105

Chapters 49–50 • Balanced Root System 106

Chapters 51–52 • Maintaining Balance 107

Chapters 53–54 • Intention To Action & Thriving 108

PART THREE • RISE 109

Chapter 55 • Your Rise 109

Chapter 56 • Mapping Your Rise 110

Chapter 57 • Your Rise in Action 119

Chapter 58 • Conclusion: From Reflection To Reality 123

BONUS CHAPTER 1: INTERNAL FAMILY SYSTEM (IFS) 129

BONUS CHAPTER 2: DARK NIGHT OF THE SOUL 135

BONUS CHAPTER 3: THE LARGER LANDSCAPE 141

Internal Family Systems (IFS)...142

Maslow's Hierarchy of Needs 143

Jungian Psychology and Shadow Work 144

Cognitive Behavioral Therapy (CBT) 145

Positive Psychology and PERMA 146

Stoicism...147

Attachment Theory 148

Somatic Awareness 149

Yoga Philosophy 150

CONGRATULATIONS...152

ABOUT THE AUTHOR 153

CONTINUE YOUR JOURNEY 154

A NOTE FROM CHANDRA LYNN

I'm happy you're here.

If this workbook found its way into your hands, something in you is ready for a shift. Maybe you're feeling stuck, stretched, or simply aware that there's more for you than the way things have been.

Root-to-Rise began as a way for me to make sense of my own life. Over time, it became a framework to help others reconnect with what matters, understand what's driving their choices, and create real change from the inside out.

I built this workbook because I needed it, and because I wanted to leave something behind. A guidebook. Not just for the people who find it now, but for my son, Kai, and for future generations who may one day want to understand themselves a little more clearly and live a little more intentionally. If this reaches you, it was meant to.

This workbook is where that change begins to take shape.

Inside, you'll find exercises, reflections, and space to apply the Root-to-Rise Framework to your own life across your five root areas: Health, Family, Relationships, Career, and Friends. Each section also stands fully on its own, though the deepest experience comes from using it alongside *Root-to-Rise: How to Love Life*.

You don't need to have everything figured out. You don't need to do this perfectly. You just need to be willing to look a little deeper and tell yourself the truth.

Think of this as a space we share. A place to check in, reflect, and realign with what you actually want your life to feel like.

Come back to it often. Your answers will evolve as you do. And make sure you sign up at glowliving.com for free updates and resources, including online diagnostic tools.

I'm here with you in this process.

Love Life.

Chandra Lynn
chandralynn.com

BEFORE YOU BEGIN

How to Use This Workbook

This workbook is organized in three phases that mirror the Root-to-Rise framework and main guide book, *Root-to-Rise: How to Love Life*. Move through them in order for the fullest experience or return to any section whenever life calls you back to it.

THE THREE PHASES

PHASE I: ROOTS - Evaluate your five life roots, understand your human needs, and clear the obstacles holding you back.

PHASE II: RESILIENCE - Build emotional strength, develop your inner guidance system, and learn to weather life's storms.

PHASE III: RISE - Step into your authentic self, create balance, define your higher purpose, and map your rise.

Tips for Getting the Most from This Workbook

☐ For the deepest experience, use it alongside *Root-to-Rise: How to Love Life* and companion journal. Each section corresponds to specific chapters and also stands fully on its own.

☐ Write honestly. No one is grading you. The more truthful you are, the more powerful your results.

☐ Don't rush. Some prompts may take days or weeks to fully answer. That's okay.

☐ Come back. Life changes, and your answers will too. Re-visit any exercise whenever you need a reset.

☐ Take the free **Hidden Forces Quiz** and **Root-to-Rise Compass** at glowliving.com during Phase I to discover which needs are driving your life and how well they're being met across your roots.

☐ Transfer key insights to your **Root-to-Rise Map** as you go. You'll find it at the back of this workbook, and you can build your digital version at glowliving.com.

☐ Whenever you want support, your **Root-to-Rise 24/7 Coach** is always available at glowliving.com — ready to answer questions or help you go deeper.

"The life you want is waiting on the other side of the work you're willing to do.
Your potential doesn't fulfill itself. You do."

RISE
RESILIENCE
ROOTS
health
family
romantic partner
career
friends

THE ROOT-TO-RISE FRAMEWORK

Root-to-Rise mirrors the way a tree grows, from the roots up. Before it reaches toward the sky, a tree invests in growing strong, deep roots that provide stability, nourishment, and resilience. Without them, even the tallest tree is vulnerable to the slightest storm. The same is true for us.

ROOTS	RESILIENCE	RISE
PHASE I	**PHASE II**	**PHASE III**
Life Root System (5)	Emotional Navigation	Authenticity
Human Needs (6)	Energy Arrows	Balance
Clearing Obstacles	Emotional Triad	Higher Purpose
Health • Family	Winds of Change	Life's Key Question
Relationships • Career	Storms • Waves	Root-to-Rise Map
Friends • Taproots	Pressure • Release	Your Legacy

What You'll Walk Away With

☐ A clear understanding of the hidden forces shaping your life

☐ A deeper relationship with your own needs, patterns, and authentic self

☐ Tools to build emotional resilience and navigate life's inevitable storms

☐ A completed Root-to-Rise Map to guide your next chapter

"By the end of this journey, you'll have a deeper understanding of the hidden forces shaping your life, and a clear path toward the future you want."

ROOT-TO-RISE INFOGRAPHIC

RISE

HIGHER PURPOSE
What do you want to be known for?

RISING UP

- Life's Key Question
- Bucket List
- Goals & Aspirations
- Accomplishments
- Connections/Relationships
- Milestone Events

BALANCING LIFE

- Yoga & Meditation
- Gratitude
- Self-care
- Prioritizing Roots

CONNECTING TO AUTHENTICITY

- Tap into Your Heart
- Aligning Others
- Your Lens

WITHSTANDING THE ELEMENTS

- Winds of Change
- Storms/Upheaval
- Grief & Loss

NAVIGATING EMOTIONS

Triad:
- Body/Mind/Spirit
- Physiology/Focus/Meaning

CLEARING OBSTACLES

- Nourishing Needy Roots
- Honoring Driving Needs
- Pain Points
- Getting Unstuck
- Fears & Limiting Beliefs
- Double Binds
- Leveraging you Tap Root

FOCUS MIND **MEANING SPIRIT**

PHYSIOLOGY BODY

RESILIENCE

LIFE ROOT SYSTEM

HEALTH/FITNESS

- Nutrition
- Food/Beverage
- Supplements
- Fitness/Exercise
- Massage/Body Work
- Wellness vs. Illness

FAMILY

- Parents
- Caregivers
- Siblings
- Partner
- In-laws
- Children
- Chosen

RELATIONSHIPS

- Self
- Romantic Partner
- Commitment
- Chemistry
- Compatibility
- Communication

CAREER

- Time & Money
- Contribution
- Heart-based/Passion vs Corporate
- Hobbies/Craft
- Who you are:
  - Strengths/Weaknesses
  - Leader vs. Worker
  - Visionary vs. Operational
  - Analytical/Data-minded

FRIENDS

- Introvert v. Extrovert Needs
- Who are they? Values alignment
- Reflection of you
- What do you offer?
- What do they offer?
- Elevate
- Support
- Experience

HUMAN NEEDS

Transcendence

- Moving past the self to serve others
- Connecting to higher purpose
- Contribution
- Sharing
- Service
- Providing

Growth

- Growing
- Pulsating energy
- Progress
- Learning
- Feeling momentum
- Advancing
- Breaking free

Intimacy

- Nurturing
- Valuing relationships
- Belonging
- Feeling passion
- Having desire
- Striving for unity
- Togetherness

Self

- Self-esteem
- Self-worth
- Significance
- Importance
- Pride
- Importance
- Perfection

Variety

- Change
- Transitions
- Storms
- Challenges
- Trauma/Crisis
- Chaos
- Variety
- New/Different
- Spice of Life
- Surprise
- Fear

Security

- Certainty
- Safety
- Rootedness
- Grounded
- Comfort
- Stability
- Predictability
- Protection
- Commitment

TAP ROOT
What feeds your soul deeply?

ROOTS

Are You Ready to Play Full Out?

Before we go any further, pause and ask yourself: How willing am I to fully commit to this process? Not just to learn the framework, but to apply it. To reflect. To journal. To do the exercises. To be honest with yourself. To take action.

Rate your willingness from 1 (not at all) to 10 (completely):
- ☐ How willing am I to challenge myself and go all in on this journey?   Score: _____
- ☐ How willing am I to show up with courage and radical honesty?   Score: _____
- ☐ How willing am I to take real action instead of staying stuck in old patterns?   Score: _____

What would it mean to play full out in this workbook?

What fear or resistance might get in your way?

MY COMMITMENT

I commit to showing up honestly, courageously, and consistently in this workbook.

Signature: _______________________________________ Date: _____________

"The willingness to show up is already an act of courage."

PHASE I: ROOTS

Before you can rise, you must tend to the ground beneath you. In this first phase, you'll explore your **Five Life Roots**, understand the **six human needs** that shape your patterns, and **clear the obstacles** standing between you and your fullest expression.

Most people spend their lives trying to grow — chasing goals, building habits, seeking happiness — without ever stopping to ask what their life is actually rooted in. They push forward without examining the ground beneath them, and then wonder why things keep falling apart, why the same patterns resurface, why success in one area never seems to translate into a sense of wholeness. The answer is almost always in the roots. When your foundational life areas are neglected, imbalanced, or quietly suffering, no amount of ambition or effort at the surface level will make up for it. You can't build a lasting rise on a shaky foundation, and you don't have to keep trying. This phase gives you the honest look most people never take.

What you'll discover here may surprise you. Some roots you thought were strong may be running on autopilot, meeting your needs in ways that cost more than they give. Others you've neglected may be the very ones quietly draining your energy, your confidence, or your sense of connection. And underneath all of it, you'll begin to uncover the deeper forces — your core human needs — that have been shaping your choices, your relationships, and your patterns all along, often without your awareness. This isn't about finding what's wrong with you. It's about finally understanding *why*, and from that understanding, deciding with intention what you want to grow.

IN THIS PHASE, YOU WILL:

- ☐ Assess the strength of each of the five life roots in your Life Root System
- ☐ Explore how your six core emotional human needs are being met (or not)
- ☐ Identify and begin clearing the patterns, fears, and beliefs holding you back
- ☐ Discover your Taproot, your deepest source of strength and purpose

"The depth of your rise will always be determined by the strength of your roots."

PART ONE • ROOTS

LIFE ROOT SYSTEM

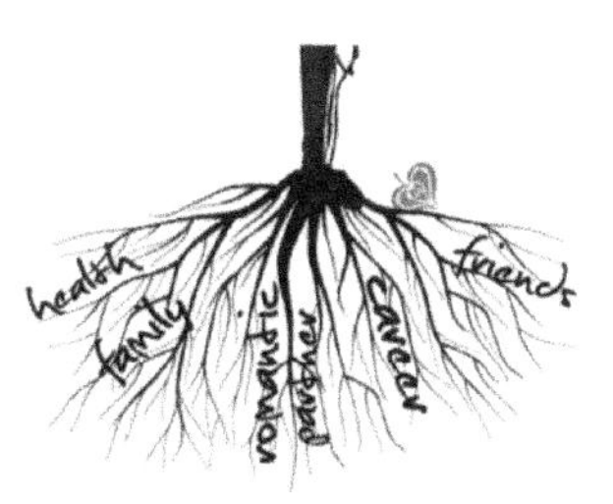

Health/Fitness

Family

Relationship

Career

Friends

Just like a tree needs strong, stable roots to grow tall and weather storms, your life needs nourishment at the foundational level. The five Life Roots — Health, Family, Relationships, Career, and Friends — represent the essential areas that support your well-being, identity, and purpose.

As you work through each root, you'll assess its current strength, identify what's thriving and what needs tending, and create a vision for what you want to grow.

As you assess each root, keep in mind that we all meet our needs — and not always in ways that serve us. Consider what each root is truly giving you right now.

Ask yourself:

☐ Where have I settled for "just okay" instead of truly thriving?
☐ What limiting beliefs are keeping me from strengthening my roots?
☐ How willing am I to challenge those beliefs and create new, healthier patterns?

THE FIVE LIFE ROOTS

Health — The Root of Vitality — your physical, mental, and emotional well-being
Family — The Root of Connection — your earliest and most formative bonds
Relationships — The Root of Love — how you give, receive, and relate to yourself and others
Career — The Root of Purpose & Prosperity — how you contribute your gifts
Friends — The Root of Support & Joy — the people who see and celebrate you

---

Why Your Roots Matter

A tree with deep, healthy roots can weather any storm. Without them, it may grow tall for a while, but it remains vulnerable. The same is true for you. When your foundational life areas are strong and balanced, you're better equipped to handle adversity, make empowered choices, and experience lasting fulfillment.

This section asks you to look honestly at each of your five roots, not to judge what you find but to understand it. Some roots will surprise you with their strength. Others may reveal neglect you hadn't fully acknowledged. Both are valuable information. The goal isn't a perfect root system. It's an honest one.

Chapter 4 • Root 1: Health – The Root of Vitality

Your health is the root from which everything else grows. Without physical and mental well-being, it's nearly impossible to show up fully in any other area of your life. This chapter asks you to assess where your health stands right now — not with judgment, but with honest awareness. Energy, sleep, movement, self-care, and your relationship with your own body all live here.

→ *For a deeper exploration of the Health root, including the real cost of neglect, a personal story, and what it means to move from survival to vitality, read Chapter 4 in Root-to-Rise: How to Love Life.*

Your Three Key Questions

These three questions are the foundation of your Root-to-Rise Map. Answer them here, for this root, while your reflection is fresh.

Question 1: What do you want?

Be specific. Not what you think you should want — what you genuinely want for this root.

Question 2: Why do you want it?

Go deeper than the obvious answer. What need would it meet? What would it make possible?

Question 3: What are you willing to do about it?

One real, honest commitment. Not a wish — an action you are genuinely willing to take.

Going Deeper into Health

Which version of health are you living today, survival or vitality?

What would thriving look like for you?

What is one small, sustainable shift you can make this week? Not from shame, but from love.

Where in your health journey do you need to ask for help or support?

★ NORTH STAR REMINDER ★

Your Health root is the foundation for how you move through the world physically, mentally, and emotionally. When it's strong, you have the energy, clarity, and resilience to rise with purpose.

Root 1: Health — Mind Map

Place "Health" at the center and branch outward. If this area of your life were flourishing, what would it look like, feel like, and allow you to experience? Capture the people, experiences, feelings, achievements, and possibilities you would love to create.

Example:

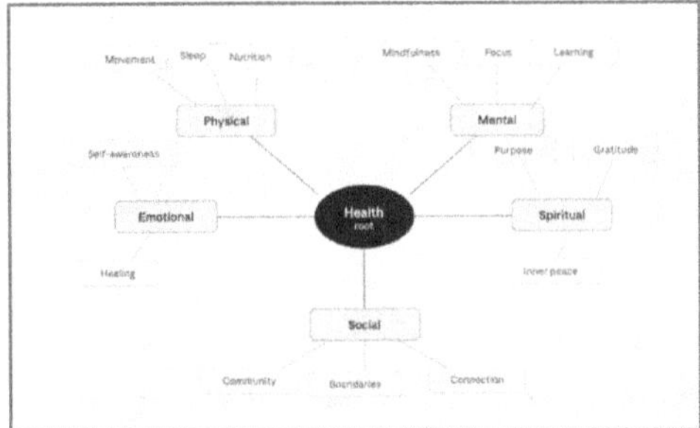

Chapter 5 • Root 2: Family – The Root of Connection

Family is often our earliest and most formative root — and for many people, the most complicated. Whether your family is a source of love and stability or of pain and unresolved history, this root shapes how you see yourself and relate to others. Here you'll look honestly at the quality of your family connections, any patterns you've inherited, and what you most want to grow in this area.

→ *For a deeper exploration of the Family root, including childhood wounds, family dynamics, and how to heal or strengthen these bonds, read Chapter 5 in Root-to-Rise: How to Love Life.*

Your Three Key Questions

These three questions are the foundation of your Root-to-Rise Map. Answer them here, for this root, while your reflection is fresh.

Question 1: What do you want?

Be specific. Not what you think you should want — what you genuinely want for this root.

Question 2: Why do you want it?

Go deeper than the obvious answer. What need would it meet? What would it make possible?

ADD TO YOUR ROOT-TO-RISE MAP

Transfer your three answers to your Root-to-Rise Map at the back of this workbook. These become the foundation for this root's section of your map.

Going Deeper into Family

Who did you have to be to get love or attention growing up? How has that shaped who you are today?

What does "family" mean to you now — not just blood, but chosen connection?

What is one relationship in your family system you want to heal, deepen, or redefine?

★ NORTH STAR REMINDER ★

Your Family root is not just part of where you came from. It's a key component of your Life Root System. Strengthening it will guide you toward greater emotional balance, connection, and legacy.

Root 2: Family — Mind Map

Place "Family" at the center and branch outward. If this area of your life were flourishing, what would it look like, feel like, and allow you to experience? Capture the people, experiences, feelings, achievements, and possibilities you would love to create. Think about connection, communication, support, traditions, belonging, and the memories you want to build together.

Chapter 6 • Root 3: Relationships – The Root of Love

This root holds your capacity for love — with a partner, and within yourself. Romantic relationships are mirrors: they show us our patterns, our needs, and our edges. Whether you're in a relationship, rebuilding after one, or choosing yourself right now, this root asks you to look at how you give and receive love, where you seek validation, and where you create or allow emotional safety.

→ *For a deeper exploration of the Relationships root, including codependency, the 51% Rule, and how to turn conflict into connection, read Chapter 6 in Root-to-Rise: How to Love Life.*

Your Three Key Questions

These three questions are the foundation of your Root-to-Rise Map. Answer them here, for this root, while your reflection is fresh.

Question 1: What do you want?

Be specific. Not what you think you should want — what you genuinely want for this root.

Question 2: Why do you want it?

Go deeper than the obvious answer. What need would it meet? What would it make possible?

Question 3: What are you willing to do about it?

One real, honest commitment. Not a wish — an action you are genuinely willing to take.

ADD TO YOUR ROOT-TO-RISE MAP

Transfer your three answers to your Root-to-Rise Map at the back of this workbook. These become the foundation for this root's section of your map.

Going Deeper into Relationships

How do you show up in romantic relationships? What pattern do you most want to change?

The 51% Rule: Are you giving at least 51% of your love and attention to yourself first? Where do you fall short?

What does emotional safety look and feel like for you? Do you create it for yourself and others?

★ NORTH STAR REMINDER ★

Your Relationships root holds your deepest desires for connection, growth, and shared purpose. Nurturing this root, within yourself and with others, aligns you with the love and partnership that reflects your truth.

Root 3: Relationships — Mind Map

Place "Relationships" at the center and branch outward. If this area of your life were flourishing, what would it look like, feel like, and allow you to experience? Capture the people, experiences, feelings, achievements, and possibilities you would love to create. Think about love, trust, intimacy, partnership, self-respect, and the qualities that create meaningful connections.

Chapter 7 • Root 4: Career – The Root of Purpose & Prosperity

Your career root is about more than income — it's about how you contribute your gifts, find purpose, and sustain yourself in the world. It encompasses your work, your sense of professional identity, and whether the way you spend your working hours aligns with who you are and what you value. This chapter asks whether your career is nourishing you or draining you — and what you most want to change.

→ *For a deeper exploration of the Career root, including entrepreneurship, creative work, and how to find purpose even in transition, read Chapter 7 in Root-to-Rise: How to Love Life.*

Your Three Key Questions

These three questions are the foundation of your Root-to-Rise Map. Answer them here, for this root, while your reflection is fresh.

Question 1: What do you want?

Be specific. Not what you think you should want — what you genuinely want for this root.

Question 2: Why do you want it?

Go deeper than the obvious answer. What need would it meet? What would it make possible?

Question 3: What are you willing to do about it?

One real, honest commitment. Not a wish — an action you are genuinely willing to take.

ADD TO YOUR ROOT-TO-RISE MAP

Transfer your three answers to your Root-to-Rise Map at the back of this workbook. These become the foundation for this root's section of your map.

Going Deeper into Career

Does your current career align with your passions and strengths? If not, what's the gap?

Define success on your own terms: What does a truly fulfilling work life look and feel like for you?

What fear or self-doubt is holding you back in your career right now?

★ NORTH STAR REMINDER ★

Your Career root reflects your values, purpose, and evolving sense of identity. When aligned, it becomes a powerful channel for contribution, growth, and fulfillment.

Root 4: Career — Mind Map

Place "Career" at the center and branch outward. If this area of your life were flourishing, what would it look like, feel like, and allow you to experience? Capture the people, experiences, feelings, achievements, and possibilities you would love to create. Think about purpose, impact, growth, creativity, abundance, freedom, and the contribution you want to make.

Chapter 8 • Root 5: Friends – The Root of Support & Joy

Friendships are one of the most overlooked roots — and one of the most important. Genuine friendships provide joy, perspective, belonging, and the kind of support that no other relationship can fully replicate. This chapter asks you to look honestly at the quality and reciprocity of your friendships, the patterns in how you connect, and what you want to cultivate here.

→ *For a deeper exploration of the Friends root, including how to navigate changing friendships, set boundaries, and invest in the connections that truly feed your soul, read Chapter 8 in Root-to-Rise: How to Love Life.*

Your Three Key Questions

These three questions are the foundation of your Root-to-Rise Map. Answer them here, for this root, while your reflection is fresh.

Question 1: What do you want?

Be specific. Not what you think you should want — what you genuinely want for this root.

Question 2: Why do you want it?

Go deeper than the obvious answer. What need would it meet? What would it make possible?

Question 3: What are you willing to do about it?

One real, honest commitment. Not a wish — an action you are genuinely willing to take.

ADD TO YOUR ROOT-TO-RISE MAP

Transfer your three answers to your Root-to-Rise Map at the back of this workbook. These become the foundation for this root's section of your map.

Going Deeper into Friends & Community

Which friendships bring out your most authentic self? Which ones require you to shrink?

Are you as good a friend to others as you want them to be to you? Where can you show up more?

Is there a friendship that needs an honest conversation, more investment, or a loving release? Explain.

★ NORTH STAR REMINDER ★

Your Friends root is a vital source of joy, connection, and resilience. It helps you weather storms and celebrate wins with people who truly see and support you.

Root 5: Friends — Mind Map

Place "Friends & Community" at the center and branch outward. If this area of your life were flourishing, what would it look like, feel like, and allow you to experience? Capture the people, experiences, feelings, achievements, and possibilities you would love to create. Think about friendship, belonging, fun, support, shared experiences, service, and the community you want to be part of.

Chapter 9 • Taproots

In order to break through the obstacles holding us back from rising, we need to summon energy from the source that feeds our roots most deeply, our Taproot. A taproot is characterized by one thick root that grows deep into the soil. It anchors the plant and draws nourishment from far beneath the surface.

In the Root-to-Rise Framework, your Taproot is your spiritual anchor. It fuels all five root areas of life and sustains your ability to meet your deepest human needs. Without it, your rise may feel directionless or easily shaken. When nourished, this foundation helps everything else flourish.

→ *For a deeper exploration of Taproots, including how to discover what truly grounds you and anchor your deepest source of strength, read Chapter 9 in Root-to-Rise: How to Love Life.*

Common Taproot Examples

- Family & Relationships — a sense of belonging, love, or responsibility
- Career or Service — finding purpose in meaningful work or creative expression
- Personal Growth — pursuing learning, healing, creating, or self-mastery
- Spirituality or Faith — drawing strength from a higher power or sacred purpose
- Contribution to Others — uplifting others through service, activism, or generosity

"When life feels overwhelming, your Taproot grounds you. It keeps you centered when you're tempted to stray and fuels your growth when you're ready to rise."

Step 1: Reflect & Journal

Use any of the following prompts to help uncover your Taproot.

What principles do I want to live by? What truly brings me joy or purpose?

What keeps me moving forward when I want to quit?

What truly feeds my soul and authentic self at the deepest level?

What impact do I want to leave behind in the world?

Step 2 & 3: Capture Your Taproot

Summarize your Taproot in a short, powerful phrase — a value, a person, a belief, or a feeling. Examples: "For my children." "I am here to serve." "Freedom and growth fuel me."

MY MAIN TAPROOT:

OTHER IMPORTANT TAPROOTS:

Pro Tip: Anchor Your Taproot Daily

Your Taproot is your most important, non-negotiable priority. To reinforce it:

- ☐ Set a daily intention tied to your Taproot
- ☐ Create a mantra (e.g., "I prioritize my health so I can show up fully")
- ☐ Use a visual cue — bracelet, phone wallpaper, or mirror note

ADD TO YOUR ROOT-TO-RISE MAP

Transfer your Taproot phrase to your Root-to-Rise Map.

★ NORTH STAR REMINDER ★

Your Taproot is the deepest truth that grounds you. It's your guiding principle, core belief, or soul-level why. When everything else feels uncertain, this is the part of you that stays steady. Come back to it often. Let it anchor your choices, fuel your growth, and remind you of who you are at your core.

Chapter 10 • Roots Recap

You've now explored each of your five Life Roots. In this section, you examined what's thriving, what needs tending, and how your core human needs are being met — or going unmet — across every area of your life.

→ *For a broader recap and reflection on all five Life Roots, including what each root gives you and how they work together as a system, read Chapter 10 in Root-to-Rise: How to Love Life.*

EACH ROOT IN REVIEW

Health — gives you the energy and strength to engage fully

Family — grounds your identity through connection and care

Relationships — deepen intimacy and self-awareness — whether with a partner or within yourself

Career — offers purpose, growth, and a platform for contribution

Friends — bring joy, support, and a sense of shared experience

Notes:

PART TWO • NEEDS

Now that you've explored your five roots, it's time to understand the hidden forces shaping how they feel. The six core human emotional needs quietly drive your decisions, relationships, and sense of fulfillment every single day.

Some of these needs may be well-met in your life. Others may be unmet, driving you toward patterns that don't serve you. Understanding your needs is how you stop reacting and start choosing.

There is something almost magical about the moment you truly understand your needs as a living key to your own interior. Suddenly, the patterns you've circled for years have a name. The relationship that always breaks down in the same place, the career move you can never quite commit to, the way you shut down or spiral when things feel uncertain. These aren't character flaws. They are unmet needs, running the show from behind the curtain. And once you can see them clearly, something shifts. You stop fighting yourself and start understanding yourself. You stop asking *what's wrong with me* and start asking *what do I need?* That single shift — from judgment to curiosity — is where real change begins. It is also where you start to free yourself from things you may have tried to fix a hundred times before, never quite knowing why they kept coming back.

The same understanding that unlocks you will also change how you move through the world with others. When someone you love is anxious, withdrawn, controlling, or impossible to please, it's easy to take it personally, or to simply feel helpless. But when you understand human needs, you begin to see beneath the behavior to what's driving it. You recognize that the person pushing you away may be desperately craving Intimacy but terrified of it. That the one who needs to be right about everything may be running on an unmet need for Self. That understanding doesn't mean excusing, it means you can finally respond instead of react. You can speak to what someone actually needs, in a way that leaves them feeling seen and nourished rather than judged. You can set boundaries without cruelty. You can love people more honestly, and more effectively, than ever before. Knowing your needs, and learning to meet them in healthy, intentional ways across your five root areas, is not just self-help. It is the code for loving life. The following pages give you the vocabulary to start reading that code, in yourself and in everyone around you.

THE SIX HUMAN NEEDS

Security — The need for safety, stability, comfort, and certainty

Variety — The need for change, challenge, novelty, and stimulation

Self — The need for significance, self-worth, and feeling valued

Intimacy — The need for connection, love, closeness, and belonging

Growth — The need to expand, learn, improve, and evolve

Transcendence — The need for purpose, contribution, and connection to something greater

Chapter 11 • Understanding Human Needs

Everything you do — every choice you make, every pattern you repeat, every relationship you keep or leave — is driven by six core human needs. These needs aren't wants or preferences. They are fundamental psychological requirements that every person on earth is trying to meet, every single day, whether they know it or not.

The six needs are: Security, Variety, Self (Significance), Intimacy (Love & Connection), Growth, and Transcendence. Each one is legitimate. Each one matters. The difference between a life that feels stuck and a life that feels alive often comes down to which needs are being met and how.

When needs are met in healthy, intentional ways, they fuel your energy, your relationships, and your sense of purpose. When they go unmet, they quietly drive the patterns, conflicts, and cycles you can't seem to break. The goal of this section is not to judge how your needs are currently being met. It is to bring them into the light so you can begin to choose.

In the following pages, you will explore each need one at a time, identifying where it shows up in your life, how it's being met (healthily and unhealthily), and what a more empowering way of meeting it might look like. Take your time with each one. These pages often reveal more than people expect.

→ *For a deeper exploration of how human needs drive your every choice and relationship, including the hidden forces behind your patterns, read Chapter 11 in Root-to-Rise: How to Love Life.*

Before You Begin: A Quick Self-Assessment

Before reading about each need in depth, do a quick gut-check. Rate how well each need feels met in your life right now on a scale of 1–10. Don't overthink it — your first instinct is often the most honest.

NEED	SCORE (1 Low–10 High)
Security — Stability, safety, consistency	
Variety — Change, stimulation, adventure	
Self (Significance) — Mattering, contributing, confidence	
Intimacy — Connection, love, belonging	
Growth — Learning, evolving, becoming	
Transcendence — Purpose, meaning, contribution beyond self	

Which score surprised you most? That's often where the most important work begins.

What does this tell you about where your energy has been going — and where it most needs to go?

Chapter 12 • Need 1: Security

Security is your need for stability, predictability, and safety. It's the foundation that allows every other area of your life to function. When this need is well-met, you feel grounded and capable. When it's unmet or overdriven, you may find yourself clinging to the familiar, avoiding necessary risks, or feeling anxious without obvious cause.

→ *For a deeper exploration of the need for Security, including how it shapes your roots, why it goes underground, and what healthy stability actually looks like, read Chapter 12 in Root-to-Rise: How to Love Life.*

LIGHT SIDE — Healthy Expression	SHADOW SIDE — When It's Overdriving
Stable routines, reliable relationships, financial safety, physical health, consistent habits, planning ahead, creating order.	Rigidity, over-controlling, fear of change, staying in situations past their time, clinging to comfort at the cost of growth.

Code Words for This Need

These are some words that signal this need is active in you:

Safe, stable, certain, protected, consistent, prepared, grounded, secure, reliable, predictable

Where does this need show up in your root areas, healthily and unhealthily?

Where is it holding you back from growth?

What is one way where you can meet your need for Security in a more empowering way?

Chapter 13 • Need 2: Variety

Variety is your need for change, stimulation, and new experience. It's what keeps life feeling alive and meaningful rather than routine and flat. When well-met, you feel engaged and energized. When unmet, life feels stagnant. When overdriven, it can create chaos, inconsistency, or an inability to commit.

→ *For a deeper exploration of the need for Variety, including what happens when it goes unmet, how it fuels restlessness, and how to channel it into aliveness, read Chapter 13 in Root-to-Rise: How to Love Life.*

LIGHT SIDE — Healthy Expression	SHADOW SIDE — When It's Overdriving
Trying new experiences, embracing change, exploring different perspectives, spontaneity, creative experimentation, travel.	Restlessness, inability to commit, constant switching, creating drama for stimulation, avoiding depth or follow-through.

Code Words for This Need

These are some words that signal this need is active in you:

Change, adventure, freedom, spontaneous, exciting, unpredictable, diverse, creative, stimulated

Where does your need for Variety energize your life?

Where does it create chaos or prevent you from going deep?

What is one healthy way to bring more meaningful variety into your routine?

Chapter 14 • Need 3: Self

Self (sometimes called Significance) is your need to feel that you matter, that your life and contributions have meaning. It's the source of healthy confidence and self-respect. When well-met, you act from genuine self-worth. When unmet, you may seek validation externally, overwork, or downplay yourself. When overdriven, it can become ego-driven or competitive.

→ *For a deeper exploration of the need for Self, including how significance gets distorted, what it means to matter without proving it, and building true self-worth, read Chapter 14 in Root-to-Rise: How to Love Life.*

LIGHT SIDE — Healthy Expression	SHADOW SIDE — When It's Overdriving
Healthy boundaries, self-confidence, setting standards, pride in work, owning your uniqueness, self-respect, authenticity.	Seeking external validation, comparison, proving yourself, needing to be right, arrogance, self-abandonment for approval.

Code Words for This Need

These are the words and phrases that signal this need is active in you:

Special, important, significant, recognized, respected, valued, unique, worthy, needed, accomplished

What does healthy self-worth feel like for you vs. seeking significance from external sources?

Where does this need show up in your root areas — healthily and unhealthily?

Where in your life are you giving away your sense of self-worth to others' opinions? What would change if you stopped?

Chapter 15 • Need 4: Intimacy

Intimacy is your need for deep connection — to be truly known, seen, and loved. It encompasses closeness with others and the relationship you have with yourself. When well-met, you feel connected and emotionally safe. When unmet, loneliness or a sense of isolation creeps in. When overdriven, it can lead to clinginess, over-sharing, or losing yourself in relationships.

→ *For a deeper exploration of the need for Intimacy, including the difference between connection and enmeshment, vulnerability, and what real belonging requires, read Chapter 15 in Root-to-Rise: How to Love Life.*

LIGHT SIDE — Healthy Expression	SHADOW SIDE — When It's Overdriving
Deep friendships, vulnerability, emotional honesty, physical affection, being fully known and accepted, genuine connection.	Codependency, over-sharing too soon, emotional distance, fear of abandonment, isolation, using others to feel complete.

Code Words for This Need

These are the words and phrases that signal this need is active in you:

Connected, loved, close, understood, seen, accepted, belonging, together, bonded, intimate

What does true intimacy feel like for you?

Where does this need show up in your root areas — healthily and unhealthily?

Where are you avoiding vulnerability or deep connection? What would it mean to let yourself be more fully known?

Chapter 16 • Need 5: Growth

Growth is your need to evolve — to learn, expand, and become more than you were yesterday. It's what keeps you engaged with your own life and prevents stagnation. When well-met, growth fuels confidence and aliveness. When unmet, you feel stuck or unfulfilled. When overdriven, it can lead to restlessness, perfectionism, or never feeling "enough."

→ *For a deeper exploration of the need for Growth, including why growth can feel threatening, how to distinguish it from restlessness, and what becoming really means, read Chapter 16 in Root-to-Rise: How to Love Life.*

LIGHT SIDE — Healthy Expression	SHADOW SIDE — When It's Overdriving
Continuous learning, embracing challenges, seeking feedback, evolving beliefs, expanding skills, self-improvement.	Overextending, never feeling "enough," using growth to avoid the present, compulsive self-improvement, burnout.

Code Words for This Need

These are some words that signal this need is active in you:

Better, learn, improve, expand, evolve, develop, progress, challenge, stretch, advance, grow

In what area of life are you growing right now in a way that feels genuinely fulfilling?

Where does this need show up in your root areas — healthily and unhealthily?

Where are you avoiding necessary growth? What would change if you leaned into it?

Chapter 17 • Need 6: Transcendence

Transcendence is your need for meaning beyond yourself — to contribute to something larger, to live with purpose, and to feel connected to something spiritual, communal, or legacy-driven. When well-met, it brings a profound sense of direction and fulfillment. When unmet, life can feel hollow even when outwardly successful. When overdriven, it can manifest as self-sacrifice or martyrdom.

→ *For a deeper exploration of the need for Transcendence, including how purpose gets buried under survival, what it means to contribute beyond yourself, and living for something larger, read Chapter 17 in Root-to-Rise: How to Love Life.*

LIGHT SIDE — Healthy Expression	SHADOW SIDE — When It's Overdriving
Service to others, spiritual practice, contributing to a cause, connection to nature, creativity as expression of the divine.	Losing yourself in a cause, martyrdom, neglecting personal needs for others, spiritual bypassing, escapism.

Code Words for This Need

These are some words that signal this need is active in you:

Purpose, meaning, serve, contribute, higher, spiritual, beyond, legacy, mission, calling, sacred, give...

What practices or experiences connect you to something greater than yourself?

Where does this need show up in your root areas — healthily and unhealthily?

How does your need for Transcendence show up in your daily life? What would it look like to honor it more fully?

Chapters 18–20 • Applying Human Needs & Needs Evaluation

Needs Evaluation by Root

Now that you understand both your five Life Roots and the six core human needs, it is time to bring them together. The following exercises ask you to assess how your needs are being met within each specific root area. Work through each root one at a time. The patterns you find here will become the foundation of your Root-to-Rise Map.

This is where the real picture emerges. You may discover that one need is being met beautifully in your career but nearly absent in your relationships — or that a need you thought was satisfied is actually being met in ways that cost you more than they give. Follow the data. It will show you exactly where to focus.

→ *For a deeper exploration of applying human needs to your root areas, including stories and how to shift toward high-quality need fulfillment, read Chapters 18–20 in Root-to-Rise: How to Love Life.*

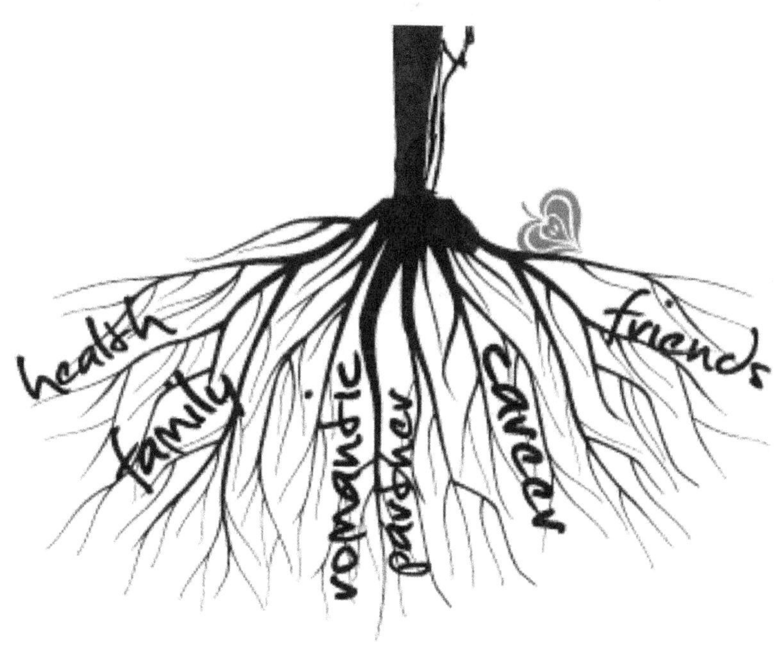

ROOT 1: HEALTH: NEEDS EVALUATION

Draw a line from 1 downward to your chosen number for each need. The longer the root, the more that need is met. Let your roots grow down the page. 1 = not fulfilled at all | 10 = completely fulfilled.

1	1	1	1	1	1
2	2	2	2	2	2
3	3	3	3	3	3
4	4	4	4	4	4
5	5	5	5	5	5
6	6	6	6	6	6
7	7	7	7	7	7
8	8	8	8	8	8
9	9	9	9	9	9
10	10	10	10	10	10
Security	**Variety**	**Self**	**Intimacy**	**Growth**	**Transcendence**

Transfer Your Scores

NEED	MY SCORE
Security	
Variety	
Self	
Intimacy	
Growth	
Transcendence	
AVERAGE (divide total by 6)	

What does your average score tell you about how well your health is supporting your life right now?

Which unmet need has the biggest impact on your physical or emotional wellbeing?

If you raised your lowest score by just two points, what would need to change in your daily life?

How Are You Meeting Your Health Needs?

For each need, list the healthy ways you're currently meeting it in this root area — and the unhealthy ways you may be defaulting to. Be honest with yourself. Awareness is the first step to change.

NEED	HEALTHY WAYS	UNHEALTHY WAYS
Security		
Variety		
Self		
Intimacy		
Growth		
Transcendence		

Healthy Examples:
Security —I go to the doctors when I know I need to.
Variety — I provide myself a variety of different workouts throughout the week: cardio, yoga, & weights.
Self — I workout to have the body I want which helps me feel confident and self-secure.
Intimacy — I ask my romantic partner to workout with me. This allows me to be vulnerable in front of them which ultimately brings us closer.
Growth — I use an app to teach me workouts I wouldn't know myself.
Transcendence — I volunteer in my community because contributing to something larger than myself gives my daily life greater meaning.

What new healthy way will you commit to for this root? _______________________________________

ROOT 2: FAMILY: NEEDS EVALUATION

Draw a line from 1 downward to your chosen number for each need. The longer the root, the more that need is met. Let your roots grow down the page. 1 = not fulfilled at all | 10 = completely fulfilled.

1	1	1	1	1	1
2	2	2	2	2	2
3	3	3	3	3	3
4	4	4	4	4	4
5	5	5	5	5	5
6	6	6	6	6	6
7	7	7	7	7	7
8	8	8	8	8	8
9	9	9	9	9	9
10	10	10	10	10	10
Security	**Variety**	**Self**	**Intimacy**	**Growth**	**Transcendence**

Transfer Your Scores

NEED	MY SCORE
Security 🌱	
Variety	
Self	
Intimacy	
Growth	
Transcendence	
AVERAGE (divide total by 6)	

What does your average score tell you about how well your family is supporting your life right now?

If you raised your lowest score by just two points, what would need to change in your daily life?

How Are You Meeting Your Family Needs?

For each need, list the healthy ways you're currently meeting it in this root area — and the unhealthy ways you may be defaulting to. Be honest with yourself. Awareness is the first step to change.

NEED	HEALTHY WAYS	UNHEALTHY WAYS
Security		
Variety		
Self		
Intimacy		
Growth		
Transcendence		

Healthy Examples:
- **Security** — I live close to family members, which assures me that they are there if I need them or they need me.
- **Variety** —When hosting a gathering, I allow my family to bring people who will fit in and because it's fun to mix it up and meet new people.
- **Self** — I share my opinions with my family, and although sometimes the differ, I feel accepted and valued.
- **Intimacy** — I schedule weekly phone calls with remote family to stay connected and to still feel close.
- **Growth** — I often ask my siblings (or chosen family) for advice in the fields I know they excel at. I respect their opinions and I want to learn from it.
- **Transcendence** — I pass along knowledge I have to my siblings, children and chosen family.

What new healthy way will you commit to for this root?______________________________________

Draw a line from 1 downward to your chosen number for each need. The longer the root, the more that need is met. Let your roots grow down the page. 1 = not fulfilled at all | 10 = completely fulfilled.

Security	Variety	Self	Intimacy	Growth	Transcendence
1	1	1	1	1	1
2	2	2	2	2	2
3	3	3	3	3	3
4	4	4	4	4	4
5	5	5	5	5	5
6	6	6	6	6	6
7	7	7	7	7	7
8	8	8	8	8	8
9	9	9	9	9	9
10	10	10	10	10	10

Transfer Your Scores

NEED	MY SCORE
Security	
Variety	
Self	
Intimacy	
Growth	
Transcendence	
AVERAGE (divide total by 6)	

What does your average score tell you about how well your relationship is supporting your life?

If you raised your lowest score by just two points, what would need to change in your daily life?

How Are You Meeting Your Needs in Relationships?

For each need, list the healthy ways you're currently meeting it in this root area — and the unhealthy ways you may be defaulting to. Be honest with yourself. Awareness is the first step to change.

NEED	HEALTHY WAYS	UNHEALTHY WAYS
Security		
Variety		
Self		
Intimacy		
Growth		
Transcendence		

Healthy Examples:
- **Security** — My partner and I regularly renew our willingness to meet each other's needs.
- **Variety** — We take many trips together to see different people and places.
- **Self** — I journal about my relationship so I have time to personally process how I feel emotionally about certain situations.
- **Intimacy** — I show physical affection to my partner every day, and don't wait for the other to initiate.
- **Growth** — My partner and I take classes together for fun and to learn new things together.
- **Transcendence** — I pass along stories from my past, resources that have helped me, and/or advice to my partner to share helpful life tools.

What new healthy way will you commit to for this root?_________________________________

ROOT 4: CAREER: NEEDS EVALUTION

Draw a line from 1 downward to your chosen number for each need. The longer the root, the more that need is met. Let your roots grow down the page. 1 = not fulfilled at all | 10 = completely fulfilled.

Security	Variety	Self	Intimacy	Growth	Transcendence
1	1	1	1	1	1
2	2	2	2	2	2
3	3	3	3	3	3
4	4	4	4	4	4
5	5	5	5	5	5
6	6	6	6	6	6
7	7	7	7	7	7
8	8	8	8	8	8
9	9	9	9	9	9
10	10	10	10	10	10

Transfer Your Scores

NEED	MY SCORE
Security	
Variety	
Self	
Intimacy	
Growth	
Transcendence	
AVERAGE (divide total by 6)	

What does your average score tell you about how well your career is supporting your life right now?

If you raised your lowest score by just two points, what would need to change in your daily life?

How Are You Meeting Your Career Needs?

For each need, list the healthy ways you're currently meeting it in this root area — and the unhealthy ways you may be defaulting to. Be honest with yourself. Awareness is the first step to change.

NEED	HEALTHY WAYS	UNHEALTHY WAYS
Security		
Variety		
Self		
Intimacy		
Growth		
Transcendence		

Healthy Examples:

- **Security** — The job I've chosen allows me to feel comfortable with where I stand financially.
- **Variety** — I've manage multiple projects because I like to focus on different areas of interest in my career.
- **Self** — I am aware of what skills I bring to the table at work. This allows me to push certain insecurities away and it provides me a sense of belonging within the company.
- **Intimacy** — I have a great relationship with my boss, and it allows me to speak openly about work and personal relations, making work-life easier.
- **Growth** — I take training courses that allow me to increase my job-related skills.
- **Transcendence** — I took on a leadership role and now coach certain individuals in certain skill areas, and it's very fulfilling.

What new healthy way will you commit to for this root?______________________________________

ROOT 5: FRIENDS: NEEDS EVALUATION

Draw a line from 1 downward to your chosen number for each need. The longer the root, the more that need is met. Let your roots grow down the page. 1 = not fulfilled at all | 10 = completely fulfilled.

Security	Variety	Self	Intimacy	Growth	Transcendence
1	1	1	1	1	1
2	2	2	2	2	2
3	3	3	3	3	3
4	4	4	4	4	4
5	5	5	5	5	5
6	6	6	6	6	6
7	7	7	7	7	7
8	8	8	8	8	8
9	9	9	9	9	9
10	10	10	10	10	10

Transfer Your Scores

NEED	MY SCORE
Security	
Variety	
Self	
Intimacy	
Growth	
Transcendence	
AVERAGE (divide total by 6)	

What does your average score tell you about how well your friends are supporting your life?

If you raised your lowest score by just two points, what would need to change in your daily life?

How Are You Meeting Your Friends Needs?

For each need, list the healthy ways you're currently meeting it in this root area — and the unhealthy ways you may be defaulting to. Be honest with yourself. Awareness is the first step to change.

NEED	HEALTHY WAYS	UNHEALTHY WAYS
Security		
Variety		
Self		
Intimacy		
Growth		
Transcendence		

Healthy Examples:
- **Security** — My friends go out every First Friday to bond, and it's nice having it scheduled so that I'm certain we'll see each other regularly.
- **Variety** — I have a wide range of friends with different interests, and I go to them for different reasons, i.e. theatre-going, fitness, travel, when I'm depressed, etc.
- **Self** — I invite my friends over for self-care nights (massage and relaxation days).
- **Intimacy** — I send cards to my friends to remind them that I think they are special.
- **Growth** — I go to weekend workshops with my friends a couple of times per year.
- **Transcendence** — If my friend needs something and I have resources or know the right people, I will connect them.

What new healthy way will you commit to for this root?_______________________________________

My Root System: Overall Composite

Using your average score from each root's Needs Evaluation, draw your overall Root System below. Shade each column up to your average score.

Health	Family	Relationships	Career	Friends
1	1	1	1	1
2	2	2	2	2
3	3	3	3	3
4	4	4	4	4
5	5	5	5	5
6	6	6	6	6
7	7	7	7	7
8	8	8	8	8
9	9	9	9	9
10	10	10	10	10

What are you noticing about the balance of your roots? Where is there the most imbalance?

Which two roots need the most nourishment right now and why? Focus on these first.

What specifically will you do to nourish these roots?

What does your life look like when these roots are thriving?

My Needs

Now that you've explored all six human needs, step back and take stock. Rate how healthily each need is currently being met in your life as a whole, not just in one root, but overall.

NEED	SCORE (1–10)	KEY INSIGHT OR NOTE
Security		
Variety		
Self		
Intimacy		
Growth		
Transcendence		

Which need is most fulfilled right now? What is working?

Which need is least fulfilled? What is one shift that would raise it by 2 points?

MY TOP DRIVING NEED:

Based on your scores

ADD THIS TO YOUR ROOT-TO-RISE MAP

PART THREE • CLEARING

Before you can rise, you have to clear the path. Strong roots can't do their work when they're tangled in weeds — old beliefs, fear-based patterns, mental clutter, and unprocessed emotion that quietly sabotage your growth.

Clearing isn't about fixing yourself. It's about making space for who you're already becoming.

IN THIS SECTION YOU WILL:

- ☐ Name the emotional weeds tangling your roots
- ☐ Identify your fear-based resistance patterns
- ☐ Release mental clutter and emotional overload
- ☐ Rewrite the limiting beliefs that keep you stuck
- ☐ Build the foundation of self-worth you deserve

"Sometimes we don't need a new plan. We need to clear
what's in the way of the one we already have."

Chapter 21 • Clearing the Way

You might be stuck not because you're broken, but because you're still carrying things you were never meant to hold. Old beliefs. Outdated identities. Unprocessed pain. Like tangled weeds, they wrap around your roots and choke the life out of your potential. The moment you can name what's in your way, you loosen its grip. Start with awareness. Not judgment. Not blame. Just awareness.

→ *For a deeper exploration of Clearing the Way — including what it truly feels like to be stuck and how to begin clearing the path for growth — read Chapter 21 in Root-to-Rise: How to Love Life.*

What is staying stuck protecting you from?

What is it costing you emotionally, creatively, spiritually?

If nothing changes, how will you feel in one year? In five years?

What pattern in your life have you clearly outgrown?

CLEARING PRACTICE

Next time you notice yourself feeling stuck or circling the same pattern, try this:

- Interrupt the loop — stand up, shake your body, take a breath, say aloud: "This pattern ends now."
- Take one small, messy step — action doesn't have to be perfect to be powerful.
- Reconnect with your why — what do you want instead of this pattern?

Chapter 22 • Fear-based Resistance

Resistance wears many disguises: perfectionism, procrastination, low standards, inconsistency, overthinking, avoidance. These patterns may look different on the surface, but underneath, they're all rooted in fear. Name any resistance patterns you recognize in yourself. What does your Inner Critic say about it, and what does your Wise Self know to be true?

→ *For a deeper exploration of Fear-Based Resistance — including how resistance disguises itself as perfectionism or procrastination, and how to release the fear beneath — read Chapter 22 in Root-to-Rise: How to Love Life.*

THE INNER CRITIC SAYS...	THE WISE SELF SAYS...

The Fear Beneath Your Pattern

For each resistance pattern below, consider whether it shows up for you and what fear drives it:

PATTERN	FEAR BENEATH IT	DOES THIS SHOW UP FOR YOU? IF SO, HOW?
Perfectionism	Fear of not being good enough	
Procrastination	Fear of failure or success	
Inconsistency	Fear of commitment or losing freedom	
Worry	Unmet needs for safety and control	

Which of these resistance patterns is most active in your life right now? How does it show up?

What is this resistance protecting you from?

What would you do – or feel – if this fear didn't exist?

What would it take to let them go? How would it help you reach your goals?

What will it cost you if you don't let go and they remain in your life for years to come?

F.E.A.R. REFRAME
Forget Everything And Run → Face Everything And Rise

Chapter 23 • Mental Clutter & Emotional Overload

Disorganization isn't just about messy spaces. Mental clutter — the unfinished tasks, unmade decisions, and constant low-grade noise in your mind — quietly drains the energy you need to rise. It's rarely about laziness. It's almost always about being overloaded. Use this exercise to name what's taking up space, and begin to clear it.

→ *For a deeper exploration of Mental Clutter & Emotional Overload — including the link between outer chaos and inner overwhelm — read Chapter 23 in Root-to-Rise: How to Love Life.*

What's Cluttering Your Mind Right Now?

List everything that feels unfinished, unresolved, or mentally heavy. Don't edit — just empty it out.

WHAT'S TAKING UP SPACE	SORT IT	FIRST STEP OR LET GO
List everything. Don't edit, just empty it out	**A** = *Act* **R** = *Release* **L** = *Later*	*What will you do, or how will you let it go?*

One Commitment

Look at your table. Circle one Act item and one Release item. What will you commit to doing or letting go of this week?

Chapter 24 • Rewriting the Script

Limiting beliefs are like invisible chains. They hold us back from reaching our full potential, often without us realizing it. These deeply ingrained thoughts shape how we see ourselves, others, and the world. But like any story, they can be rewritten.

→ *For a deeper exploration of Rewriting the Script — including how limiting beliefs formed and practical tools for replacing them with an empowering new story — read Chapter 24 in Root-to-Rise: How to Love Life.*

Three-Column Rewrite

In the left column, write old limiting beliefs. In the middle, trace where they came from. In the right column, write a new empowering story.

OLD STORY	WHERE IT CAME FROM	NEW EMPOWERING STORY

A Letter to Your Younger Self

The three-column exercise helps you see a limiting belief clearly. Writing a letter to your younger self helps you *release* it. Your most stubborn beliefs didn't come from nowhere. They were formed by a younger version of you who was trying to make sense of something hard. Writing to that younger self isn't about blame or pity. It's about compassion and closure. *There's no right way to write this letter. Let it be honest, even if it's messy.*

In your letter, consider:

- How old were you when this belief took root? What was happening?
- What did you need to believe back then to feel safe or make sense of things?
- What do you know now that your younger self couldn't have known yet?
- What would you want them to hear from someone who loves them?

Dear younger me,

Chapter 25 • Hidden Emotional Traps

Some of the deepest blocks aren't beliefs or fears, they're binds. Moments where both options feel wrong. Stay or go. Speak up or stay safe. Need others or stay independent. These hidden traps keep you circling the same place without knowing why.

→ *For a deeper exploration of Hidden Emotional Traps — including how internal conflicts form and how to find a path beyond them — read Chapter 25 in Root-to-Rise: How to Love Life.*

Name Your Trap

Is there a situation in your life right now where both options feel like a loss? Describe it.

The Underlying Needs in Conflict

Look at the two sides of your bind. What need does each side protect? (Use your knowledge of the six needs.)

- ☐ Staying / Option A protects my need for: _______________________
- ☐ Leaving / Option B protects my need for: _______________________

A Third Option

What might be possible if you didn't have to choose between the two? Write freely — don't edit.

Chapter 26 • Foundation of Self-Respect

Before you can rise, you have to believe you deserve to. Self-respect isn't arrogance. It's the quiet, steady knowledge that you matter, your needs are valid, and your life is worth building intentionally.

→ *For a deeper exploration of Foundation of Self-Respect — including the roots of "not enough" thinking and how to build the self-worth to rise — read Chapter 26 in Root-to-Rise: How to Love Life.*

The "Not Enough" Audit

In what areas of your life do you most often feel "not enough"? Check all that apply and add your own.

- ☐ Professionally
- ☐ In relationships
- ☐ As a parent / family member
- ☐ In my body or appearance
- ☐ Financially
- ☐ Other:

Where Did It Come From?

Choose one "not enough" from above. When did you first start believing this about yourself? What was happening?

The Counter-Truth

Write one statement that directly counters this belief — something true about you that this belief has been blocking you from seeing.

Chapter 27 • Clearing the Path

You have done the work of this phase. You have named your patterns, faced your fears, questioned your beliefs, and begun to understand what has been holding you back. Before you move forward, take a moment to consolidate what you've uncovered.

→ *For a deeper exploration of Clearing the Path — including how to consolidate your insights and prepare for what comes next — read Chapter 27 in Root-to-Rise: How to Love Life.*

Your Clearing Recap

Complete each statement:

☐ The limiting belief I most want to release is:

☐ The fear beneath it is:

☐ The "not enough" story I'm ready to let go of is:

☐ One pattern I am choosing to break is:

What You're Making Room For

Clearing isn't just about removing. It's about creating space. What do you want to grow in the space you've just cleared?

"You can't unsee what you now know. Awareness itself is transformation."

PHASE I • CLOSING REFLECTION
Clearing Complete

You've done significant work in this phase. You've looked at your roots honestly, explored the needs driving your patterns, and begun clearing what's been standing in your way. That takes courage.

What is the most significant thing you cleared or discovered in Phase I?

What pattern, belief, or story are you consciously leaving behind?

What do you feel ready for now that you've done this work?

MY PHASE I AFFIRMATION

Write a short, powerful statement of affirmation or intention to carry into Phase II:

"Clearing isn't about fixing yourself. It's about making space
for who you're already becoming."

PHASE II: RESILIENCE

You've strengthened your roots. Now it's time to test them. Life will always bring change, challenge, and unexpected storms. Resilience is how you meet them without being uprooted.

Resilience isn't a personality trait you either have or don't. It's a practice that can be learned, strengthened, and called upon exactly when you need it most. And it matters more than most people realize, because without it, even the strongest roots can't protect you from being knocked sideways by life. Anxiety and depression are two of the most common ways an under-resourced nervous system responds to the weight of unmet needs, unprocessed pain, and relentless pressure. They are not signs of weakness. They are signals from your inner world telling you that something needs attention. But left unaddressed, they quietly erode your ability to show up, to connect, to take risks, to feel joy. They keep you stuck in loops that shrink your world smaller and smaller, until the life you want feels not just distant, but impossible.

I know this terrain personally. There were seasons of my life when getting out of bed felt like a negotiation, when the simplest decisions felt impossible, and when the version of myself I believed in felt very far away. What I learned is that those seasons didn't mean I was broken. They meant I was depleted. My roots had weakened. My needs had gone unmet for too long. And I had never been taught how to work with my own emotional landscape rather than fight it. That's what this phase gives you. Not a cure. A compass.

This phase is your way back. Building emotional resilience means learning to work *with* your inner landscape instead of against it. You will interrupt the patterns that drag you down, regulate your nervous system in real time, and move through hardship without losing yourself in it. It means developing the tools to face fear without being paralyzed by it, to grieve without drowning, to bend under pressure without breaking. The work in this phase won't eliminate life's difficulties. Nothing can. What it will do is change your relationship to them so that when the storms come, and they will, you are not helpless. You are grounded, resourced, and ready to rise.

IN THIS PHASE YOU WILL:

- ☐ Master The Triad — your real-time tool for shifting your emotional state
- ☐ Understand and break depressive patterns with compassion
- ☐ Become intentional about the energy you send and receive
- ☐ Navigate the five elements: Winds of Change, Storms, Grief, Pressure, and Letting Go
- ☐ Build the practices that steady you — before, during, and after life's hardest seasons

PART ONE • EMOTIONS
Navigating Emotions

Emotions are not problems to solve. They are messengers guiding you toward what's aligned, and alerting you when something needs attention. In this section, you'll build your emotional navigation toolkit: The Triad, Energy Arrows, your personal peak state rituals, and your Emotional Guidance System.

Healthy emotional navigation isn't about avoiding feelings or rushing to fix them. It's about understanding your emotional responses and using them as guides.

THE EMOTIONAL NAVIGATION TOOLKIT

The Triad — Shift your emotional state by adjusting Physiology, Focus, and Meaning

Energy Arrows — Understand the invisible emotional signals you broadcast and receive

Happy Dance — Reclaim joy and create peak state rituals that work for you

Emotional Fitness — Build the self-awareness to show up fully in your relationships

Emotional Guidance System — Use your emotions as a compass, not a crisis

---

"You don't build resilience by avoiding hard things. You build it by surviving them and choosing to stay standing. And growing from them is how you rise."

Triad:
Physiology-Focus-Meaning

Balance:
Body-Mind-Spirit

Of all the tools in Root-to-Rise, The Triad is the one to return to again and again, especially in moments of overwhelm, conflict, or self-doubt. Three forces create every emotion you experience, whether you're aware of them or not.

→ *For a deeper exploration of Navigating Emotions, including how The Triad works in both directions and how to use it to build emotional fluency, read Chapter 28 in Root-to-Rise: How to Love Life.*

What makes The Triad so powerful is that it works in both directions. Your emotional state is always being shaped by these three forces. The question is whether you're doing it consciously or not. When you're anxious, your body contracts, your focus narrows to everything that could go wrong, and your mind builds a story that confirms the fear. Each element feeds the others, pulling you deeper into the state.

The Triad is also one of the most powerful tools you have for breaking the patterns that anxiety and depression create. Both states hijack all three elements simultaneously: collapsing the body, narrowing the focus, and generating stories that feel absolutely true but are built entirely from fear.

The Triad doesn't ask you to pretend those stories aren't there. It asks you to interrupt the loop at its most accessible point and create just enough space for something different to emerge. Over time, working with The Triad builds a kind of emotional fluency: the ability to recognize what state you're in, understand what's driving it, and deliberately shift it. Not perfectly. Not always easily. But consistently enough to change your state, your day, your life.

THE THREE ELEMENTS

Physiology (Body) — How are you breathing? What's your posture? Are your muscles tense or relaxed? The way you hold your body sends instant signals to your nervous system, either reinforcing the stress response or guiding you back to safety.

Focus (Mind) — What are you paying attention to? Your focus acts like a flashlight, and whatever you shine it on gets bigger. Change your focus, and you change the emotional weight of the moment.

Meaning (Spirit) — What story are you telling yourself? The language you use and meaning you attach to your experiences is where emotions are born. Change the story, shift the emotion.

Triad Practice: Right Now

Use the table below to check in with all three elements of your Triad in this current moment. Then identify a shift you can make in each.

PHYSIOLOGY (Body) How am I using my body?	**FOCUS (Mind)** What am I paying attention to?	**MEANING (Spirit)** What story am I telling myself?

Real-Time Reset: The Centered Mindset Shift

When you're feeling off-center, use these prompts to recalibrate:

- Body: Stand tall, take 3 deep belly breaths, open your chest, lift your gaze.
- Mind: Ask yourself, "What else is true right now? What am I grateful for?"
- Spirit: Reframe the story. What empowering meaning could I assign to this moment?

Describe a recent situation where your emotional state got away from you. Walk through how you could have applied The Triad:

Which element of the Triad is hardest for you to shift? Why do you think that is?

"When emotions feel overwhelming, shift just one element of the Triad.
And watch how the others follow."

Chapter 29 • Breaking Depressive Patterns

Depression is one of the hardest emotional states we face. Using The Triad, you can interrupt depressive patterns — not by bypassing the pain, but by creating doorways out of it.

→ *For a deeper exploration of Breaking Depressive Patterns, including personal stories, the Feel + Deal = Heal framework, and how to reclaim your power, read Chapter 29 in Root-to-Rise: How to Love Life.*

★ *Important: This content supports emotional awareness and is not a substitute for therapy or clinical treatment. If you're experiencing persistent or severe depression, please reach out to a licensed therapist or doctor.*

FEEL + DEAL = HEAL

Yes, feel the emotion. Let the tears come. Name the fear. Sit with the pain. Then ask:
What is this feeling trying to show me? What's the lesson, or even the gift, in this?

My Depressive Pattern Audit

Notice how your body and mind change when depression or low mood starts. Fill in each column:

PHYSIOLOGY (Body) How am I using my body?	FOCUS (Mind) What am I paying attention to?	MEANING (Spirit) What story am I telling myself?

What are 3 physical actions that immediately shift your state when you feel low? (e.g., walk outside, stretch, play music)

Write one mantra or in-CAN-tation that counters your most persistent low-mood thought:

Chapter 30 • Energy Arrows

Every moment, whether we realize it or not, we're sending out energy arrows — emotional signals that affect others for better or worse. They're not visible, but they're profoundly felt. By becoming more conscious of the energy you broadcast, you step into your power as a creator of connection, calm, and joy.

→ *For a deeper exploration of Energy Arrows — including the invisible emotional frequencies you broadcast and how to become intentional about your energy — read Chapter 30 in Root-to-Rise: How to Love Life.*

ARROW TYPE	ENERGY BROADCAST	EFFECT ON OTHERS
Uplift Arrow	Joy, encouragement, warmth	Boosts morale, invites connection
Grounding Arrow	Calm, steadiness, presence	Eases tension, promotes safety
Discharge Arrow	Anger, frustration, irritation	Can cause tension, defensiveness
Neediness Arrow	Anxiety, insecurity, fear	May trigger distancing or people-pleasing
Withdrawal Arrow	Sadness, shutdown, flatness	Creates distance, emotional disconnection
Inspiring Arrow	Passion, vision, aliveness	Energizes, motivates, sparks possibility

Which arrow type do you most commonly broadcast? In which situations?

Which arrow do you most want to send more intentionally? What would that require of you?

My Energy Arrows

Your arrows are shaped by your Triad: your body, your focus, and the meaning you assign.

When you self-regulate, you don't just protect your own peace. You become a source of calm and clarity for everyone around you.

PEOPLE / SITUATIONS THAT ENERGIZE ME	PEOPLE / SITUATIONS THAT DRAIN MY ENERGY

The Arrow Reset in 60 Seconds

- Notice — Pause and name the energy you're currently emitting (tense, flat, warm, etc.)
- Breathe — Three deep breaths, exhale longer than inhale, to signal calm to your nervous system
- Shift Focus — Ask: "What's one empowering thought I can focus on right now?"
- Choose a New Arrow — Set an intention: "I bring ease into this space." or "I'm sending grounded warmth."

What does your default arrow look and feel like when you're under stress? How do others experience it?

What energy do you want to be known for bringing into a room? Write your personal arrow intention:

YOUR ARROW INTENTION

Complete this statement and carry it with you:

"Every time I walk into a room, I want people to feel

_______________________________."

"Awareness is the moment you notice where your energy is flowing. Responsibility is the choice to redirect it toward the life you want to create."

Chapter 31 • Happy Dance

When was the last time you truly let loose and allowed joy to take over? A happy dance isn't just a silly gesture — it's a scientifically backed way to shift your state. Movement releases endorphins, lowers cortisol, boosts dopamine, and deepens your connection to the present moment. Joy is not optional. It's essential. And it's yours to reclaim.

→ *For a deeper exploration of the Happy Dance — including why joy is essential (not optional) and how to reclaim peak states in your everyday life — read Chapter 31 in Root-to-Rise: How to Love Life.*

WHY WE HOLD BACK OUR HAPPINESS
- Feeling self-conscious about expressing joy openly
- Suppressing happiness to match someone else's lower energy
- Waiting for a "big enough" win before allowing celebration
- Not giving yourself permission to feel good without earning it

When did you last genuinely celebrate something, big or small? What happened?

What holds you back from expressing joy freely? Be honest:

My Peak State Ritual

List 5 things that instantly shift your state to positive. These are your personal joy triggers and peak state activators, i.e. music, calling a friend, etc.

1. ____

2. ____

3. ____

4. ____

5. ____

Create your Happy Dance playlist — list you favorite songs that make you move:

CELEBRATE YOURSELF: 3 RECENT WINS

Acknowledge your progress — big or small:

1. ____

2. ____

3. ____

Chapter 32 • Emotional Fitness for Relationships

Emotional fitness is the foundation of the relationships we create. The stronger your emotional fitness, the healthier and more fulfilling your relationships will be. It's not just about who you're with; it's about who you are within them.

→ *For a deeper exploration of Emotional Fitness for Relationships — including all ten steps and how each one shapes the depth of your connections — read Chapter 32 in Root-to-Rise: How to Love Life.*

The 10 Steps of Emotional Fitness

Self-Awareness	Recognize your emotions, triggers, and relationship patterns so you can respond consciously instead of reacting impulsively
Emotional Regulation	Manage conflict and stress without lashing out or shutting down
Empathy	Tune into what others feel; listen with an open heart and validate feelings
Healthy Communication	Express yourself clearly, listen actively, avoid criticism and defensiveness
Conflict Resolution	Navigate conflict with maturity; seek solutions and repair connection
Boundaries	Respect your own limits and the limits of others without overextending
Resilience	Weather life's challenges without breaking your relationships in the process
Positive Mindset	Focus on what's right in your relationships instead of obsessing over imperfections
Accountability	Own your mistakes without self-loathing; take responsibility and repair
Growth Together	See relationships as a space for mutual evolution, not just comfort

Which of these 10 steps is your strongest? Which needs the most growth?

What emotional pattern do you most want to change in how you show up for others?

Chapter 33 • Emotional Guidance System

Your emotions are not problems to solve, they're a compass. When you feel joy, love, or peace: this is aligned. When you feel anger, sadness, or anxiety: something needs attention. The goal isn't to leap from despair to joy overnight. It's to reach for the next best feeling, one rung at a time.

→ *For a deeper exploration of your Emotional Guidance System — including how to use your emotions as a compass rather than a crisis — read Chapter 33 in Root-to-Rise: How to Love Life.*

Emotion Spectrum Map

Map your most common emotional states on this spectrum. Mark where you tend to live day-to-day with an X, and where you want to be with a ♡:

CONSTRICTED	TRANSITIONING	EXPANSIVE
Fear • Shame • Despair Anger • Anxiety • Numb	Frustration • Overwhelm Doubt • Neutral • Hope	Gratitude • Joy • Love Peace • Confidence • Awe

Think about an emotion that's been dominant for you lately. What is it trying to show you?

If this emotion had a voice, what would it say you need more of — or less of — right now?

What shift — in your body, your focus, or your story — would bring you relief or clarity today?

"I trust my emotions to guide me, not define me. I honor every feeling
as a messenger, and I meet each one with compassion."

PART TWO • ELEMENTS

You've done powerful work strengthening your emotional roots. Now, you're ready to test them in the real storms of life. Change, crisis, grief, stress, and the art of letting go will challenge every part of who you are. They will also reveal a deeper strength you didn't know you had.

THE FIVE ELEMENTS OF RESILIENCE

Winds of Change — Life's transitions — career pivots, relationship endings, unexpected turns

Storms of Life — Crises that strike without warning and test your emotional, financial, and physical strength

Crashing Waves — Grief and loss — mourning someone, something, or a part of yourself

Pressure Systems — The daily stress that, left unchecked, accumulates into burnout and overwhelm

Releasing to Rise — The sacred act of letting go — of resentment, old identities, and what no longer serves you

---

"Storms will come. The question is: how will you navigate them?"

Chapter 34 • Withstanding the Elements

Storms don't ask if you're ready. They arrive uninvited during transitions, crises, grief, pressure, the slow ache of letting go. This section of the workbook doesn't ask you to avoid those seasons. It asks you to meet them better equipped than before.

The five elements you'll explore — Winds of Change, Storms, Crashing Waves, Pressure Systems, and Releasing to Rise — are the most testing passages of any life. They are also, consistently, where the most profound growth happens.

→ *For a deeper exploration of Withstanding the Elements — including how to prepare for life's hardest seasons and what the five elements reveal about your own resilience — read Chapter 34 in Root-to-Rise: How to Love Life.*

Before you begin, take stock of where you are right now.

Which element are you currently navigating?

- ☐ Winds of Change — a transition or major life shift
- ☐ Storms — a crisis or unexpected disruption
- ☐ Crashing Waves — grief or loss of some kind
- ☐ Pressure Systems — sustained stress or overwhelm
- ☐ Releasing to Rise — something I need to let go of
- ☐ I am in a season of relative calm and working proactively

What does "withstanding" look like for you right now?

Not enduring, but meeting this season with intention. What would that require of you?

CHAPTER 35 • WINDS OF CHANGE

Chapter 35 • Winds of Change

Life's transitions: career pivots, relationship endings, unexpected turns

---

Change is inevitable. Sometimes we welcome it. Sometimes it blindsides us. But no matter how it arrives, change asks us to move, to stretch, to grow. The Winds of Change show up in countless ways: a career shift, a divorce, a new stage of life, a change in identity or calling.

Change challenges one of our deepest human needs: Security. When life shifts unexpectedly, the mind naturally clings to what feels familiar, even if that familiarity no longer serves us.

→ *For a deeper exploration of the Winds of Change — including how to anchor through life's transitions and who you are becoming on the other side — read Chapter 35 in Root-to-Rise: How to Love Life.*

What winds of change are currently moving through your life — big or small?

What emotions are coming up for you around this change? (Fear, excitement, grief, relief?)

Navigating Change with Resilience

- Anchor to your core values — when everything around you is shifting, your values become your compass
- Honor what you're leaving behind — gratitude and grief can coexist
- Focus on what remains steady — your skills, your character, your resilience
- Reframe fear as excitement — "This isn't fear. This is the energy of transformation."
- Stay open to who you're becoming — who you were yesterday does not define who you must be tomorrow

What is still true about you, no matter what changes around you?

What strengths have past life transitions already revealed in you?

What new possibilities are calling to you through this change, even if they scare you a little?

"When the winds of change begin to blow, remember: roots provide stability, and growth requires movement.

Chapter 36 • Storms of Life

Crises that strike without warning and test your emotional, financial, and physical strength

Storms hit hard and fast, forcing you into survival mode and making it difficult to think clearly or trust that you'll make it through. They arrive without warning and demand everything you have. A health crisis. Sudden job loss. Financial collapse. The end of a relationship you believed was permanent. Unlike the slow drift of the Winds of Change, storms don't give you time to prepare. But no storm lasts forever. And every one you've survived has prepared you for this one.

→ *For a deeper exploration of Storms of Life — including how to survive a crisis, find your anchors, and emerge with strength you didn't know you had — read Chapter 36 in Root-to-Rise: How to Love Life.*

ANCHORS FOR THE STORM

- Reach out for support — you don't have to do this alone
- Prioritize self-care — even minor acts of care matter during crisis
- Take it one step at a time — just focus on the next right action
- Control what you can, release what you can't
- Remind yourself: "This will pass." The storm may be strong, but so are you

---

What storm are you currently moving through, or still healing from?

Where are you stronger today because of past storms you've survived?

What anchors — people, practices, beliefs — can you rely on when life feels most uncertain?

What small act of self-care or courage can you take today to steady yourself?

Chapter 37 • Crashing Waves

Grief and loss — mourning someone, something, or a part of yourself

Sometimes what follows a storm isn't relief. It's grief. Crashing Waves are different. They don't arrive with force. They rise from within. Grief is one of the deepest and most universal human experiences. It doesn't follow a predictable or linear path. Grief isn't something we "get over." It's something we learn to carry. And what makes it so hard is that it's also a testament to love. We grieve deeply because we loved deeply.

Grief isn't just about death. It can be the loss of a marriage, a friendship, a dream, a phase of life, or a version of yourself.

→ *For a deeper exploration of Crashing Waves — including how to grieve fully, carry love forward, and find meaning in loss — read Chapter 37 in Root-to-Rise: How to Love Life.*

What — or who — are you grieving right now? (All forms of loss are valid here.)

What emotions have surfaced most strongly during this grief?

In what ways can you honor what was lost — the love, the dream, or the chapter that ended?

Exercise: Writing a Letter to Your Loss

Write a letter to the person, relationship, or version of yourself that you've lost. Express what you didn't get to say. Acknowledge what you miss. Share the ways they shaped you.

LOVE DOESN'T END WITH LOSS

How can you consciously carry forward the best of what you've lost? Write one way their memory lives on in how you show up:

Chapter 38 • Pressure Systems

The daily stress that, left unchecked, accumulates into burnout and overwhelm

---

Stress isn't just an inconvenience; it's a silent thief of joy, energy, and well-being. When prolonged, it creates a state of "dis-ease" in the body. Radical self-care is not a luxury. It is a necessity.

→ *For a deeper exploration of Pressure Systems — including the hidden cost of chronic stress and how radical self-care becomes your greatest act of resilience — read Chapter 38 in Root-to-Rise: How to Love Life.*

Recognize the Signs of Chronic Stress

Check any that currently apply to you:

☐ Frequent headaches or muscle tension

☐ Fatigue or trouble sleeping

☐ Feeling overwhelmed, irritable, or emotionally numb

☐ Low motivation or lack of joy

☐ Digestive issues or appetite changes

☐ Depression, anxiety, or social withdrawal

The Triad for Stress: My Nature Walk Check-In

When stress builds, use the Triad as your reset. Even a short walk can be transformative. Check in:

PHYSIOLOGY (Body) How am I using my body?	FOCUS (Mind) What am I paying attention to?	MEANING (Spirit) What story am I telling myself?

What is your most reliable practice for releasing stress? When did it last work for you?

What would "radical self-care" actually look like in your life right now? Be specific:

What are you willing to do for self-care on a regular basis?

GRATITUDE AS AN ANTIDOTE

List 3 things you are genuinely grateful for right now, even if life is hard:

1. ____

2. ____

3. ____

Chapter 39 • Releasing to Rise

The sacred act of letting go of resentment, old identities, and what no longer serves you

True resilience isn't about holding onto everything. It's about knowing what to release so you can move forward with strength and clarity. We hold on because part of us believes "This protects me." But over time, the cost adds up: your energy, your peace, your identity, your growth, and most of all…your freedom.

→ *For a deeper exploration of Releasing to Rise — including the art of forgiveness, how to identify what you're carrying, and what becomes possible when you let it go — read Chapter 39 in Root-to-Rise: How to Love Life.*

The Backpack Exercise

Imagine you've been carrying a heavy backpack. Every item inside is something you've been holding: a grudge, an old identity, a painful memory, an outdated belief, a role you've outgrown.

WHAT I'M CARRYING (List it)	READY TO RELEASE? (Yes / Not yet)

What have you been holding that was never really yours to carry?

If you set down the heaviest thing in your backpack, what would become possible?

FORGIVENESS AS RELEASE

Forgiveness doesn't mean what happened was okay. It means you're no longer willing to carry it.

Is there someone — or something — you are ready to forgive? Write their name or describe it:

"Letting go isn't about losing. It's about transforming.
It's the space where grief and love meet."

Self-Care During Difficult Times

When life gets hard, self-care is the first thing we drop, and the most essential thing to protect. These are the practices that steady you before, during, and after life's storms. Commit to yours now, so they're ready when you need them.

#	I COMMIT TO THIS PRACTICE DURING DIFFICULT TIMES?	
1.		
2.		
3.		
4.		
5.		
6.		
7.		
8.		

Which of your self-care practices is most critical to protect, even when life gets chaotic?

MY STORM SURVIVAL KIT

When life feels overwhelming, I will:

Call: ____

Practice: ____

Remember: ____

Release: ____

Chapter 40 • After the Storm

Life has a way of shaking us. Sometimes gently, sometimes without mercy. The storm is only part of the story. What matters just as much is what you carry out of it. And more often than not, what you carry out is strength you didn't know you had.

→ For a deeper exploration of After the Storm — including how to consolidate your resilience, integrate what you've survived, and carry your strength forward — read Chapter 40 in Root-to-Rise: How to Love Life.

KEY REMINDERS FROM THE ELEMENTS

- Change is inevitable, and how you meet it is a choice
- Crisis doesn't define you — your response does
- Grief is not a problem to fix — it's a process to honor
- Stress is a signal, not a life sentence
- Letting go and forgiveness are signs of powerful self-trust, not weakness

What is one storm you've come through that showed you how strong you really are?

What practice or mindset shift helps you stay most grounded during change?

What are you still carrying that it's time to release?

Closing Reflection

What shifted most in you during the Resilience phase?

What emotional pattern are you leaving behind as you move into Phase III?

What new strength have you claimed through this work?

→ *The depth of each storm season — what it costs, what it teaches, and how to find meaning on the other side — is explored fully in Chapters 34–40 of Root-to-Rise: How to Love Life. Return to those chapters any time you need more context, more story, or a reminder of why this work matters.*

You've rooted deeply. You've built resilience. Now it's time to rise.

This is the phase I love most to witness in people. Not because the hard work is over—it rarely is—but because this is where it begins to show. Where the clearing creates space for something meaningful to grow. Where resilience transforms into purpose. Where the lessons, insights, and strengths you've developed start to take shape in the world around you.

What follows is not just reflection. It is a plan. A vision. An opportunity to consciously design a life that aligns with your values, honors your needs, and supports the person you want to become. In this section, you'll move beyond simply understanding yourself and begin applying what you've learned to create meaningful change.

You'll also explore one of our deepest human needs: transcendence. While security, connection, growth, and fulfillment are important, many people discover that lasting meaning comes from contributing to something greater than themselves. Whether through your work, relationships, creativity, service, leadership, or daily acts of kindness, transcendence invites you to share your gifts in ways that positively impact others.

Growth begins below the surface, but every strong root eventually gives rise to something beautiful and valuable that can serve others. Just as a tree draws nourishment through its roots before offering shade, fruit, beauty, and shelter, we too are called to grow beyond ourselves and contribute in ways that are uniquely our own.

In this section, you'll complete your Root-to-Rise Map. This map serves as your personal blueprint for growth and fulfillment. By bringing together everything you've discovered about your roots, resilience, needs, values, and vision, you'll create a clear picture of where you're headed and why it matters.

Your map is meant to evolve as you do. Return to it often. Refine it as life changes. Let it remind you that growth is not a destination, but a lifelong journey of becoming, contributing, and rising.

"Growth begins below the surface, but every strong root eventually gives rise to something beautiful and valuable that can serve others."

PART ONE • AUTHENTICITY

Authenticity is about living in alignment with who you truly are — your values, desires, and purpose — rather than conforming to external expectations. It's about shedding the masks, releasing the roles that don't serve you, and embracing the version of yourself that feels the most honest, free, and fulfilled.

Research shows that people who score higher in authenticity report greater life satisfaction, self-esteem, and well-being, and lower levels of anxiety and depression.

Rising into authenticity is one of the most courageous things a person can do. It asks you to stop performing a version of yourself and start inhabiting the real one, with all its edges, desires, and quiet truths. This section is your invitation to do exactly that.

THE FOUNDATIONS OF AUTHENTICITY

Self-Awareness — Understanding your values, beliefs, passions, strengths, and weaknesses

Honesty — Acknowledging your true desires, fears, and needs without self-censorship

Living Your Values — When your actions reflect your deeply held beliefs, fulfillment follows

Letting Go of Pretense — The courage to be seen exactly as you are — flaws, quirks, and all

Evolving Over Time — Your authenticity isn't fixed. Honor who you are today and who you're becoming

Self-Compassion — Accepting yourself completely — strengths and imperfections alike

---

"Your most authentic life begins the moment you stop asking who you should be and start honoring who you are."

Chapter 41 • Connecting to Authenticity

When you live out of alignment with your authentic self, you'll always feel like something is missing. You might have the "perfect" job, the "ideal" relationship, or a life that looks great from the outside — yet inside, you feel disconnected, restless, or trapped. True fulfillment comes from honoring your own needs, not from checking off boxes created by someone else's definition of success.

→ For a deeper exploration of Connecting to Authenticity — including the research behind authenticity and how to align your life with who you truly are — read Chapter 41 in Root-to-Rise: How to Love Life.

Signs of Misalignment — Check Any That Apply

- ☐ Feeling unfulfilled at work or in relationships, even when things "look right"
- ☐ Suppressing your desires, opinions, or needs to please others
- ☐ Persistent stress, anxiety, or a sense that something is "off"
- ☐ Exhaustion from performing roles that don't reflect who you really are
- ☐ Feeling unseen, or like the real you hasn't been shown to the world

Where in your life are you living according to someone else's script? What would your own version look like?

What are the three core values you most want your life to reflect right now?

Who will you be when you stand unapologetically in your truth? What will you create?

"You can't seek approval and authenticity at the same time. Your truth is your power."

Chapter 42 • Unveiling the Masks

We are born knowing exactly who we are. But as we grow, we become shaped, and sometimes distorted, by our environment. These masks often feel safer than revealing our true selves, but over time they create a disconnect that leaves us feeling unfulfilled and out of sync.

→ *For a deeper exploration of Unveiling the Masks — including the childhood roots of the masks we wear and how to shed them — read Chapter 42 in Root-to-Rise: How to Love Life.*

Which Masks Have You Worn?

- ☐ The Peacemaker — always avoiding conflict, suppressing your own needs to keep the peace
- ☐ The Achiever — earning love and worth through success and external accomplishments
- ☐ The Caretaker — ignoring your own needs to keep others happy and feeling needed
- ☐ The Chameleon — adapting to fit any room, losing your sense of self in the process
- ☐ The Performer — showing only the highlight reel; afraid to be seen as flawed or struggling
- ☐ The Shrinking Violet — making yourself small so others feel more comfortable

Which of these masks do you most recognize in yourself? When did you first start wearing it, and for who?

What are you afraid will happen if you take it off?

PERMISSION TO BE FULLY YOU

Say yes to:

- ■ Speaking up, even when your voice shakes
- ■ Showing up, even if you feel different from everyone else
- ■ Saying no, even if others expect yes
- ■ Living boldly, even if it breaks the mold

Chapter 43 • Self-Confidence & Your Wild Side

At our core, we all have a wild, unapologetic energy — a vibrant part that is bold, creative, and expressive. Yet many of us have buried this part under layers of self-doubt and the need for external validation. The moment you recognize you've been reinforcing limiting beliefs, you gain the power to rewrite them.

→ For a deeper exploration of Self-Confidence & Your Wild Side — including why we dim ourselves and how to reclaim bold, authentic self-expression — read Chapter 43 in Root-to-Rise: How to Love Life.

WHERE I PLAY SMALL	WHAT IT'D LOOK LIKE TO FULLY SHOW UP

What parts of yourself have you been hiding to keep others comfortable? What would it mean to reclaim them?

Visualization: Meet Your Wild Self

Close your eyes. Picture a version of you who is completely free, uninhibited, playful, bold, radiant. What are you doing? How do you speak? What energy surrounds you? Let that version of you speak.

What does your fully unleashed, unapologetic self look and feel like? Describe them:

What limiting belief most prevents you from living that way? Rewrite it here:

Old belief:

New empowering story:

CONFIDENCE CHALLENGE THIS WEEK
Choose one small act of boldness. Write it down. Do it.

Chapter 44 • Lightening Up

One of the most powerful ways to lighten up is by reconnecting with your Inner Child, the part of you that craves play, creativity, and spontaneity. This part laughs without hesitation, dances without self-consciousness, and finds joy in the simplest things. When ignored, life can feel like an endless to-do list. When honored, your Inner Child reconnects you with joy, freedom, and ease.

→ For a deeper exploration of Lightening Up — including how to reconnect with your Inner Child and invite more joy, play, and freedom into your life — read Chapter 44 in Root-to-Rise: How to Love Life.

What did you love doing as a child that you've stopped doing as an adult?

What messages did you receive growing up about being playful, loud, or silly? How did that shape you?

What would joy look like if you removed all guilt, fear, or shame from it?

JOY WITHOUT OUTCOME

List 3 things you can do purely for joy this week — with no agenda, no product, no performance:

1. ____

2. ____

3. ____

Letter to Your Inner Child

On the next page,write a letter to your Inner Child. Speak directly to the younger version of you. What does your Inner Child need to hear from you today? What are you ready to offer them?

Dear Inner Child,

Chapter 45 • Standing True

As you evolve, people may ask you to do things that no longer align with your truth. Standing in your truth is a gift, not just to yourself, but to others. By holding your own, you model self-respect and invite others to reflect on their own patterns.

→ *For a deeper exploration of Standing True — including how to navigate relationships that resist your growth and the cost of holding back — read Chapter 45 in Root-to-Rise: How to Love Life.*

LIFE'S THREE KEY QUESTIONS

These questions are not just journal prompts, they are a compass. Return to them whenever you feel stuck, unclear, or off course:

1. What do I truly want? (Set aside what others expect. This is your truth.)

2. Why do I want it? (This is your fuel. Your Taproot. Your why.)

3. What am I willing to do to get it? (Willingness is the bridge between intention and action.)

What do I truly want in this season of my life?

Why does it matter to me at the deepest level?

What am I genuinely willing to do — and give up — to create it?

Is there a relationship or role I've been holding onto past its time? What would "standing true" look like there?

Chapter 46 • Authenticity in Friendships

Friendships naturally evolve. The real challenge isn't that they change; it's that we often fail to communicate those changes. Authenticity in friendships means showing up honestly and openly, even when things are shifting.

→ *For a deeper exploration of Authenticity in Friendships — including why friendships shift and how to show up honestly when they do — read Chapter 46 in Root-to-Rise: How to Love Life.*

The Intimacy Ladder

Not all relationships are meant to live at the same level of closeness. Place the key people in your life on the ladder below — those you're closest to at the top, those at more of a distance lower down.

Top Rungs	Deepest trust — fully known, emotionally intimate, reciprocal
Middle Rungs	Close but not always confided in — caring, consistent, valued
Lower Rungs	Acquaintances and community — meaningful but not primary

Is there a friendship you're holding onto out of habit, guilt, or history rather than genuine mutual nourishment?

What truth do you need to express to a friend, even if it's uncomfortable?

What does a healthy, deeply aligned friendship look and feel like to you now?

Chapter 47 • Intimacy & Vulnerability

True intimacy starts within. It begins with how deeply you know, accept, and nurture yourself before extending that same depth of connection to others. Vulnerability is the bridge that leads to intimacy — and for many of us, that bridge feels dangerous to cross.

→ *For a deeper exploration of Intimacy & Vulnerability — including the role of self-talk, the vulnerability leap, and how to be more fully known — read Chapter 47 in Root-to-Rise: How to Love Life.*

Intimacy with Yourself First

Your inner dialogue is your closest life partner. It's with you every moment of every day.

How positive is the way I talk to myself

If this inner voice were a person, would I want them as my best friend? Why/Why Not?

What would it take to become my own best friend?

What is the cost of staying the same? What does my life look like in 1, 3, 5, or 10 years if nothing changes?

Deepening Intimacy with Yourself

The depth of intimacy you can experience with others is almost always limited by the depth of intimacy you have with yourself. This exercise is about closing the gap between who you perform for the world and who you actually are when no one is watching.

What parts of yourself do you most often hide — from others, or even from yourself? (Old wounds, desires, fears, parts you were told were "too much"?)

When you imagine being completely known — no editing, no performing, no managing how you're perceived — what comes up? Fear? Relief? Both?

What is one truth about yourself that you rarely say out loud — not because it's shameful, but because you've never felt safe enough to claim it fully?

"A fulfilling life is built on alignment—between what you believe, what you value, and how you choose to live.""

The Vulnerability Leap

Vulnerability doesn't mean oversharing — it means taking small, courageous steps toward openness. Check any that feel like a growth edge for you right now:

☐ Express my needs out loud rather than assuming others will know them

☐ Share a fear or insecurity with someone I trust

☐ Be honest about my emotions rather than brushing them aside

☐ Stay present in a difficult conversation instead of shutting down

☐ Let someone see me when I'm not "fine" or performing strength

Where in your life are you avoiding vulnerability? What's the underlying fear?

What would it mean to let yourself be more fully known by someone you love?

Chapter 48 • Living Your Truth

7-Day Authenticity Challenge

Living authentically is a transformative journey that begins with self-awareness and unfolds into a life aligned with who you truly are. You've done the inner work. Now it's time to bring your truth into motion — one courageous act at a time.

→ *For a deeper exploration of Living Your Truth — including how authenticity creates lasting transformation and the courage it takes to stand in your truth — read Chapter 48 in Root-to-Rise: How to Love Life.*

DAY	MY AUTHENTIC ACT	HOW IT FELT
Day 1		
Day 2		
Day 3		
Day 4		
Day 5		
Day 6		
Day 7		

At the end of each day, ask yourself: What did I do today that was true to me, and how did that feel?

After 7 days: What shifted? What became easier? What do you want to carry forward permanently?

PART TWO • BALANCE

Now that you've gained clarity on who you are and what it means to live authentically, the next step is creating balance in your daily life in a way that supports your Life Root System. How do you structure your days in a way that nourishes your energy, well-being, and personal growth?

Balance isn't about perfection or giving equal time to everything. It's about presence, intentional adjustment, and aligning your life with what truly nourishes you at the deepest level.

THE FOUR PILLARS OF BALANCE

Physical Health — Strength, nourishment, and movement your body needs to function optimally

Mental Well-Being — Clarity, focus, and mindset that shape your perception and resilience

Emotional Resilience — Your ability to process, regulate, and express emotions in healthy ways

Spiritual Connection — A sense of purpose, presence, and alignment that fuels your inner life

---

"Balance isn't about doing it all. It's about doing what matters
in a way that serves your well-being."

Chapters 49–50 • Balanced Root System

One of the biggest misconceptions to release: balance means giving equal time and energy to everything. That's not just unrealistic, it's exhausting. Life is full of change, interruptions, and shifting needs. Balance is a living practice, a flexible dance with your priorities that shifts as you grow.

→ *For a deeper exploration of balance — including the myth of perfect balance and how to cultivate stability across your root system — read Chapters 49–50 in Root-to-Rise: How to Love Life.*

What part of your life feels most imbalanced right now?

Which of the four pillars — Physical, Mental, Emotional, Spiritual — is most neglected? What's the cost?

My Balanced Week

Design a sample week that gives intentional nourishment to each root area. Aim to combine needs where you can (e.g., a hike with a friend meets both physical and emotional needs).

DAY	NOURISHMENT ACTIVITIES (What's on your plate?)
Monday	
Tuesday	
Wednesday	
Thursday	
Friday	
Saturday	
Sunday	

Chapters 51–52 • Maintaining Balance

Life rarely sticks to the script. Unexpected demands pop up. Priorities shift. Maintaining balance long-term means learning how to adjust in real time, protect your energy, and be brutally honest about what truly matters. It also requires you to ask yourself: What are you willing to commit to, and what do you need to release right now?

→ *For a deeper exploration of maintaining and sustaining balance — including holistic practices for lasting harmony — read Chapters 51–52 in Root-to-Rise: How to Love Life.*

Burnout Prevention Check-In

Check any warning signs currently active for you:

- ☐ Feeling resentful about things I once loved
- ☐ Exhaustion even after resting
- ☐ Overcommitting to obligations that no longer inspire me
- ☐ Consistently procrastinating the things that matter most
- ☐ Spreading myself too thin across too many commitments
- ☐ Giving from empty — nothing left for myself

My Non-Negotiable Rituals

These are the anchors that keep you grounded, no matter what life throws at you. When self-care and reflection become built-in habits, they don't get pushed aside when life gets busy.

RITUAL TYPE	MY SPECIFIC PRACTICE
Morning Ritual	
Evening Ritual	
Weekly Reset	
Physical Practice	
Spiritual/Soul Practice	

Chapters 53–54 • Intention To Action & Thriving

Balance doesn't just happen. It's something you create by being intentional about how you spend your time and energy. If it's not scheduled, it's not real.

→ *For a deeper exploration of Intention to Action — including how to schedule a life that truly feeds your roots — read Chapters 53–54 in Root-to-Rise: How to Love Life.*

Step 1: What Would Make Each Root Area a 9 or 10? Fill in your answers:

ROOT AREA	TO FEEL LIKE A 9 OR 10, I NEED:	SCHEDULE IT (WHEN?)
Health		
Family		
Relationships		
Career		
Friends		
Personal Growth		

Step 2: Weekly Accountability Check-In

At the end of each week, ask yourself these three questions:

What went well? Where did I show up for myself?

What felt unbalanced? Where did I drift?

What needs to shift for next week?

PART THREE • RISE

Chapter 55 • Your Rise

You've cultivated your roots. You've strengthened your foundation. Now, it's time to stretch, expand, dream bigger, and live in full alignment with your purpose.

This is the moment the whole framework has been building toward. Your roots are stronger. Your resilience is deeper. You have shed masks, found your balance, and begun living with more authenticity than when you started. Rising isn't a destination you arrive at — it's a way of being you grow into.

→ For a deeper exploration of Your Rise — including what it means to step into your highest potential and begin bearing fruit for the world — read Chapter 55 in Root-to-Rise: How to Love Life.

THE RISE EQUATION

Rising Up = Strong Foundation + Personal Goals + Higher Purpose + Meaning + Joy

---

Before you complete your Root-to-Rise Map in the next chapter, take a moment to mark this threshold. You have earned it.

How have you changed?

Look back at who you were when you began this workbook. What is genuinely different now — in how you think, feel, or show up?

What does your rise look like?

Not the perfect version. The real one. What does a life you love — lived on your terms — actually feel like day to day?

What are you most ready to claim?

Complete this statement: I am rising into ____

> "Rising isn't just about achieving goals. It's about becoming the person you were always meant to be."

Chapter 56 • Mapping Your Rise

This is your personal blueprint, a declaration that you will not settle. You will rise with intention, meaning, and joy. Work through each section below with depth and honesty. When complete, you can transfer the key phrases to your visual Map template at the end of this chapter. When you're ready to take it further, build your digital Root-to-Rise Map at glowliving.com. If you want support while mapping, your Root-to-Rise 24/7 Coach is there to guide you anytime.

→ *For a deeper exploration of Mapping Your Rise, including a step-by-step guide to completing your Root-to-Rise Map as a living blueprint, read Chapter 56 in Root-to-Rise: How to Love Life.*

1. MY TAPROOT — What grounds and anchors me

2. NORTH STAR: HEALTH

What do I want for my Health root?

Why do I want it? (My deepest motivation — my fuel)

What am I willing to do about it? (Concrete, honest actions)

ROOT-TO-RISE MAP • FAMILY

What do I want for my Family root?

Why do I want it? (My deepest motivation — my fuel)

What am I willing to do about it? (Concrete, honest actions)

"Ultimately, rising is about transcending your own needs. Once your roots are strong, you begin to bear fruit: sharing gifts, wisdom, and contributions that nourish others."

NORTH STAR: RELATIONSHIPS

What do I want for my Relationships root?

Why do I want it? (My deepest motivation — my fuel)

What am I willing to do about it? (Concrete, honest actions)

ROOT-TO-RISE MAP • CAREER

What do I want for my Career root?

Why do I want it? (My deepest motivation — my fuel)

What am I willing to do about it? (Concrete, honest actions)

ROOT-TO-RISE MAP • FRIENDS

What do I want for my Friends root?

Why do I want it? (My deepest motivation — my fuel)

What am I willing to do about it? (Concrete, honest actions)

ROOT-TO-RISE MAP • CONTINUED

3. MY TOP DRIVING NEED — From the 6 human needs — which am I cultivating now?

4. MY FAVORITE MANTRA — A phrase I want to live by

5. MY TOP SUPPORTERS — Who uplifts, challenges, and believes in me?

6. MY AUTHENTIC SELF DESCRIPTORS — 3–5 words that describe my truest self

7. MY LIFE'S KEY QUESTION — What question will guide my empowered future?

8. MY TOP MILESTONES — Key moments of growth and proof of my strength

9. MY GOALS & ASPIRATIONS — What I deeply desire to accomplish in the next year (and beyond)

10. MY TOP BUCKET LIST ITEMS — Experiences and adventures I'm committed to living

11. MY MOST IMPORTANT LIFE LESSONS — Profound truths I've learned

12. WHAT I AM GRATEFUL FOR — People, experiences, and lessons I'm most thankful for

13. MY HIGHER PURPOSE — In five words or less: what am I here to do?

Transfer the key elements of your answers to your visual map on the next page. An example is provided following the blank template.

ROOT-TO-RISE MAP

HIGHER PURPOSE

RISE

LIFE'S KEY QUESTION

AUTHENTIC SELF DESCRIPTORS

TOP SUPPORTERS

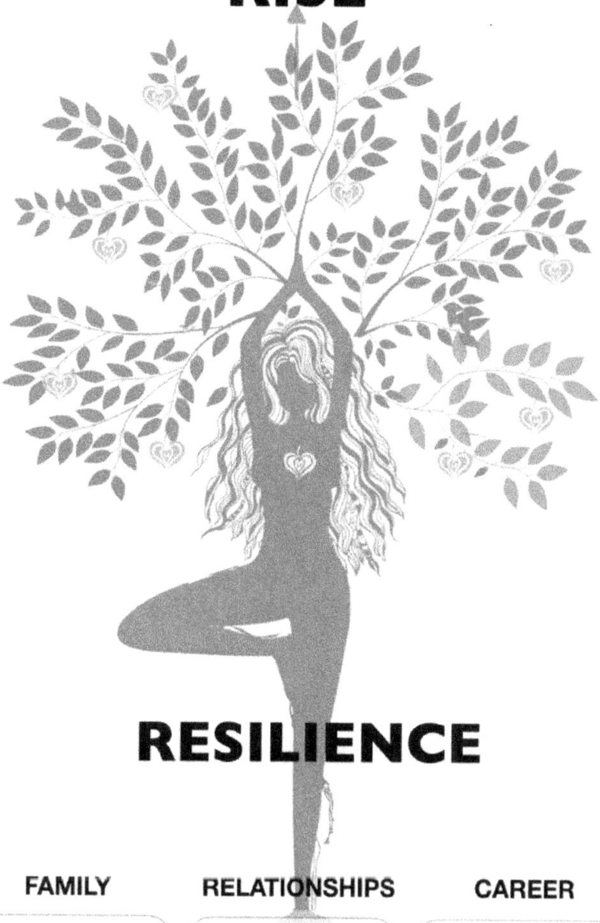

FAVORITE MANTRA

TOP DRIVING NEED

TOP MILESTONES

GOALS & ASPIRATIONS

TOP BUCKET LIST

TOP LIFE LESSONS

GRATEFUL FOR

RESILIENCE

TOP GOALS/VISIONS

HEALTH	FAMILY	RELATIONSHIPS	CAREER	FRIENDS
What I want:				
Why I want				
What I will do for it:				

ROOTS

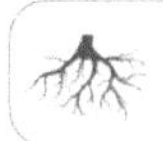

TAP ROOT

ROOT-TO-RISE MAP

HIGHER PURPOSE
I help people love life.

RISE

RESILIENCE

LIFE'S KEY QUESTION
Will this make me feel happy and fulfilled?

AUTHENTIC SELF DESCRIPTORS
Loving
Giving
Joyful

TOP SUPPORTERS
Cleo
Tiana
See:
Acknowledgements

FAVORITE MANTRA
I'm enough.

TOP DRIVING NEED
Connection/Love

TOP MILESTONES
Raised a son
Created RTR
World Travel

GOALS & ASPIRATIONS
Peak Health
Financial Freedom
Help 1M people

TOP BUCKET LIST
Travel extensively
Invest in a minority biz

TOP LIFE LESSONS
Don't boil the ocean.
No storm lasts forever.

GRATEFUL FOR
Myself and the loves in my life.
Nature.

TOP GOALS/VISIONS

	HEALTH	FAMILY	RELATIONSHIPS	CAREER	FRIENDS
What I want:	Clean bill of health. Athletic body fat %	To heal past hurts with my parents and feel connected	A committed partnership built on love, trust and shared vision.	Successfully self-employed. Time for creative projects.	Tight friend group for consistent connection & fun
Why I want it:	To prevent illness. To look fit. To be able to adventure.	I want to be clean of the past and in good place when they pass	To share my love, experience connection, and have support.	Prospect for clients. Deliver high results. Learn new skills.	To have more fun, adventure, joy and support
What I will do for it:	Exercise 4x+/week Eat whole foods Monitor weight and fat %	Go to therapy to heal myself first. Open up to them.	Discuss my needs Co-create a relationship vision.	Message 2x+ prospects per week. Learn new tech solutions.	Invite friends for activities 2x+/week. Plan trips together. Tell them they are special to me often.

ROOTS

TAP ROOT
The love of my son and helping him love life.

Chapter 57 • Your Rise in Action

Your rise isn't just a dream on paper. It's a way of living, loving, and leading every day. To embody your rise means showing up in alignment with your North Star, even when life gets messy. It means anchoring into something greater, letting your values guide your actions, and remembering that the way you live today is the legacy you leave behind.

→ *For a deeper exploration of Your Rise in Action — including spiritual anchoring, living your legacy, and embodying your rise every day — read Chapter 57 in Root-to-Rise: How to Love Life.*

Spiritual Anchoring

In every journey of growth, there comes a point when self-effort alone no longer feels like enough. You crave connection — not just to others, but to something greater. Spirituality helps us rise by reminding us: you're not rising alone.

PRACTICES THAT ANCHOR THE SPIRIT

- Meditation or Breathwork — quiet the noise and reconnect to your inner being
- Nature Immersion — walk among trees, sit near water, watch the sky
- Creative Expression — art, dance, and music as spiritual channels
- Prayer or Gratitude Rituals — speak to something beyond yourself with reverence
- Silence and Stillness — space for intuition and inner knowing to emerge
- Sacred Community — surround yourself with others on the journey of awakening
- Rituals and Ceremony — lighting candles, journaling by moonlight, celebrating transitions

---

What helps me feel most spiritually connected and grounded?

How do I want to invite more sacredness or spiritual practice into my daily life?

Living Your Legacy Today

The greatest lie we tell ourselves is that we have more time. Legacy is about alignment, not just achievement. It's the story people tell about how you lived, how you loved, and how you made them feel.

If I knew I only had one year left to live, what would I prioritize differently, starting this week?

How do I want to be remembered? What values do I want to embody?

**Complete this statement: "When I'm living fully, I'm embodying ________________,
________________, and ________________.**

Challenge: Write Your Own Eulogy

Imagine you've lived the most courageous, creative, love-filled life imaginable. What would people say about you? What moments would define your story? What qualities would they remember? Let this vision guide how you show up today.

MY LEGACY PROJECT

One thing I will start, create, or offer this week as an act of legacy:

What is the single most important shift you are committing to as you step into your rise? Not a list — the one thing that, if you actually did it, would change everything.

Who do you need to become to sustain this rise? Describe the version of you who is already living it.

My Rise in Action: 90-Day Commitment

Your rise is not someday. It's now. The path from vision to embodiment happens through consistent, values-driven action — one courageous step at a time. Use this page to anchor your commitments for the next 90 days.

LIFE ROOT	MY 90-DAY COMMITMENT	FIRST STEP (THIS WEEK)
Health		
Family		
Relationships		
Career		
Friends		
My Taproot		

Who will you share this commitment with and check in monthly? _______________________________

Chapter 58 • Conclusion: From Reflection to Reality

Do you remember the version of you who opened this workbook? The one who was ready for a shift, but maybe not quite sure what that meant yet? Look how far they came. Look how far you came. The person who opened this workbook and the person who is closing it are not the same, and that difference is entirely yours. You made it happen.

Completing this workbook is not an end; it's a beginning. The self-awareness you've gained is now your compass. The tools you carry are seeds that will continue to grow. And your Root-to-Rise Map is your living blueprint, a reminder that you are never truly lost as long as you stay connected to your truth.

Now is the time to live your legacy. Not someday when conditions are perfect. Today, exactly as you are.

What is the single most transformative insight from this entire journey?

What are you leaving behind as you step into your next chapter?

What declaration do you want to make to yourself as you close this workbook?

How Far You've Come

Before you close this workbook, take a breath. Look back. Not to dwell, but to witness. The person who opened the first page was already brave enough to begin. The person holding it now has done something most people never do — they went inward, did the honest work, and chose to rise.

This final section is your chance to honor that journey. Not to perform growth, but to truly see it.

My Growth Mirror

In each area below, reflect honestly on where you started and where you stand now. Even small shifts are real shifts.

AREA	WHERE I STARTED	WHERE I AM NOW
My Roots		
My Emotions		
My Authenticity		
My Balance		
My Purpose		

When you compare where you started to where you are now, what stands out most?

"Growth isn't always smooth, but it's always worth it."

My Aha Moments

An aha moment is more than an insight. It's a before-and-after point. A moment when something you'd been circling finally clicked, when a truth you'd been avoiding became impossible to ignore, or when a pattern you'd been living suddenly had a name.

These are the moments that change the trajectory. Honor them.

PHASE	MY BIGGEST AHA MOMENT
Phase I: Roots	
Phase II: Resilience	
Phase III: Rise	
Overall Journey	

Which single aha moment surprised you the most? What did it unlock for you?

Which insight do you most want to remember one year from now? Write it as a declaration:

What I Now Know to Be True

Every chapter you read, every prompt you answered, every honest moment you sat with, all added up to something. This is your chance to distill it. What are the ten most important things this journey taught you about yourself, your life, and how you want to show up in the world?

Don't overthink it. Write what comes first. Those are the truths that landed deepest.

#	WHAT I NOW KNOW TO BE TRUE
1	
2	
3	
4	
5	
6	
7	
8	
9	
10	

Of everything you've learned, which truth will be hardest to keep living? What will help you stay committed to it?

My Growth Story

Growth isn't linear. It doesn't always feel triumphant. Sometimes it feels like confusion or grief or the quiet discomfort of outgrowing something you used to love. That's still growth. In fact, that might be the most important kind.

What is the most significant way you have grown as a person through this work?

What pattern, belief, story, or role did you leave behind — and what did you step into instead?

I left behind:

I stepped into:

Who do you see when you look in the mirror now, compared to when you started?

What is one promise you will make to yourself — right now — about how you will continue to rise?

Going Deeper

These bonus chapters are here for you if you feel called to go deeper. By now, you've done meaningful work. You've explored your roots, begun to understand your needs, and started to shift how you show up in your life. That alone is powerful. And growth doesn't stop here. It expands as you continue to live what you're learning.

As I developed the Root-to-Rise Framework, I found that it naturally connects with other powerful ways of understanding ourselves, such as approaches that explore our inner patterns, the harder seasons of life, and the deeper questions about meaning and purpose. These chapters are an extension of that. They're here to support you if you're curious about how this work integrates with other philosophies and modalities.

These chapters are for the reader who wants to go further, feels the framework connecting to something larger, and wants to follow that thread. If something in you is curious, lean in.

Each chapter meets you in a different place:

- One helps you understand the different parts of yourself that can either support or block your growth.

- One offers guidance for the moments when life feels uncertain, heavy, or hard to make sense of.

- One zooms out to explore the bigger picture—how this work connects to a broader, more conscious way of living.

You can come back to them when something in your life shifts. You may find one resonates immediately, while another makes more sense later. That's part of the process. Take what supports you. Come back when you're ready for more. And trust that your growth is unfolding in exactly the way it's meant to.

Sign up for new content and updates at glowliving.com

How Internal Family Systems Works with Root-to-Rise

You have done a lot of honest work in this workbook. You have looked at your roots, explored your emotional needs, and begun clearing what has been holding you back.

And yet, if you are anything like most people, there may be moments when you sit down to do this work and something inside resists. A voice that says this is pointless. A heaviness that makes it hard to begin. A part of you that would rather stay busy, stay comfortable, or stay exactly where you are. That resistance is not a problem. It is actually important information.

This bonus chapter introduces a tool called Internal Family Systems, or IFS, and shows you how it works alongside the Root-to-Rise Framework. You do not need any prior knowledge of IFS to use it. Think of it as one more way to understand the emotional landscape of your life, from the inside out.

What Is Internal Family Systems?

Internal Family Systems is a model developed by Dr. Richard Schwartz that offers a simple but profound idea: we are not one unified self. We are made up of many parts.

Think about a moment when you knew you wanted to make a change — eat better, set a boundary, have a hard conversation — and something inside you pulled in the opposite direction. That tension is not weakness or lack of discipline. It is two parts of you, both trying to help, just in different ways.

IFS teaches that every part of us (even the ones that seem difficult or self-destructive) developed for a reason. Parts are protective. They formed in response to earlier experiences when they were needed. They are not the enemy. They are asking to be understood.

The Core Idea

At your center is what IFS calls the Self.

The Self is calm, grounded, curious, and compassionate. It is the wise part of you that already knows what you need. When you lead from Self, you can relate to your parts with understanding rather than judgment.

The goal is not to eliminate your parts. It is to build a relationship with them so they no longer have to run the show alone.

How IFS Connects to Root-to-Rise

In the Root-to-Rise Framework, your life is shaped by five roots and six core emotional needs. When those needs go unmet, patterns show up — in your choices, your relationships, your health, your sense of self.

IFS helps you understand where those patterns live on the inside.

Root-to-Rise	IFS	Together They Show You
Six Emotional Needs	Parts trying to meet needs	Why you do what you do
Five Life Roots	Where parts show up in life	Which areas need tending
Clearing obstacles	Unburdening protective parts	How to release old patterns
North Star / Purpose	Self-led living	Who you are when you rise

Understanding Your Parts

Parts often show up as feelings, thoughts, impulses, or inner voices. Some common ones you may recognize:

The Protector — The part that keeps you from taking risks. It may look like procrastination, perfectionism, or staying busy. It is trying to keep you safe.

The Critic — The part that tells you that you are not enough. It may sound harsh, but it originally formed to help you improve or fit in.

The Pleaser — The part that puts others first, sometimes at the cost of your own needs. It learned that harmony felt safer than truth.

The Achiever — The part that links your worth to your productivity. It is trying to help you feel significant and secure.

The Avoider — The part that shuts down, distracts, or goes numb when things get hard. It learned that not feeling was sometimes easier than feeling too much.

You may recognize some of these. You may have others that are uniquely yours. None of them are problems to fix. They are parts to get curious about.

Working with Your Parts

You do not need to be a therapist or trained coach to begin working with your parts. The practice is simply one of noticing, getting curious, and responding with compassion rather than judgment.

When a part shows up — resistance, anxiety, the urge to scroll instead of journal — try this:

1 **Notice it without judgment**

Something in me feels resistant right now. Something in me wants to quit. Something in me is afraid.

2 **Get curious about it**

What is this part feeling? What is it trying to protect me from? What does it need me to know?

3 **Thank it**

This part has been working hard, possibly for a long time. Acknowledging it shifts the dynamic from conflict to conversation.

4 **Lead from Self**

Ask the part if it would be willing to step back just a little — not go away, just make room. Then see what becomes possible.

A Note on Language

Instead of saying:

"I am anxious" or "I am stuck"

Try saying:

"A part of me feels anxious" or "A part of me is stuck"

This small shift creates distance between you and the experience. It reminds you that this is a part of you, not the whole of you. And it opens the door to curiosity rather than identification.

Root-to-Rise Daily Alignment Worksheet
Supporting Your Inner Ecosystem

Use this worksheet as a daily or weekly practice to check in with yourself across all dimensions of the Root-to-Rise Framework. It takes about ten to fifteen minutes. Come back to it whenever you need to reset, realign, or simply slow down enough to listen.

---

1. ARRIVE

One word to describe how I feel right now:

Where do I feel this in my body?

---

2. PARTS CHECK-IN (Your Inner Weather)

Notice what parts are present right now. You do not need to name them perfectly. Just notice.

Part 1 — What is this part feeling?

What is it trying to help me with?

What is it afraid would happen if it didn't show up?

Part 2 (optional):

Part 3 (optional):

3. ROOT SCAN (Where is this showing up?)

Check any roots that feel activated, heavy, or in need of attention right now:

- ☐ **Health** — body, energy, mental and emotional wellbeing
- ☐ **Family** — family dynamics, caregiving, inherited patterns
- ☐ **Relationships** — romantic connection, intimacy, how you show up with others
- ☐ **Career** — work, income, purpose, creative expression
- ☐ **Friends / Community** — belonging, support, social connection

Notes — what feels most alive in this root right now?

4. NEEDS ALIGNMENT (What do I truly need?)

Check any needs that feel most unmet or most activated today:

- ☐ **Security** — safety, stability, predictability
- ☐ **Variety** — change, lightness, relief, stimulation
- ☐ **Self** — respect, autonomy, validation, significance
- ☐ **Intimacy** — connection, understanding, being truly seen
- ☐ **Growth** — progress, expansion, forward movement
- ☐ **Transcendence** — purpose, meaning, trust in something larger

My primary need right now:

What would it feel like if this need were truly met?

5. ONE SUPPORTIVE ACTION

What is one small, realistic action I can take today to support this need? Keep it simple and doable.

6. SELF-LEADERSHIP (Your North Star)

Complete this sentence:

"I see that part of me that feels... and I want you to know... Today, I will support myself by..."

Evening Reflection (Optional)

Return to this at the end of your day. A few minutes is enough.

What felt supportive today?

What triggered me?

Which part showed up the most?

What did I need that I can give myself tomorrow?

"You are not your patterns. You are the one who can notice them."

When Your Life No Longer Fits

There may come a moment in your life when what once felt certain no longer holds. The routines that grounded you begin to feel empty. The relationships that once felt easy start to feel distant or unclear. The work you have built, the identity you have carried, the roles you have played all begin to feel misaligned. And you may not know why.

From the outside, your life might still look stable. You may be doing everything you are supposed to do, and inside, something is shifting. Something deeper is asking to be seen.

This is what many have called a dark night of the soul.

It is not a sign that you have lost your way. Often, it is the moment when you can no longer continue living in a way that is not true for you.

The Experience Few People Talk About

A dark night of the soul rarely arrives with a clear announcement. More often, it unfolds quietly.

It can feel like:

1. A loss of energy for things that once mattered
2. A sense of emptiness or disconnection
3. Emotional waves without a clear source
4. Questioning your purpose, relationships, or direction
5. A subtle or overwhelming feeling of something's off, but I can't name it

You may try to push through it, fix it quickly, or judge yourself for feeling this way — and the feeling remains. This is not something to bypass. It asks to be experienced and understood.

What Is Actually Happening Beneath the Surface

In the Root-to-Rise Framework, your life is supported by five roots: Health, Family, Relationships, Career, and Friends. Each of these roots is nourished by your emotional needs. During this phase, something essential begins to shift. The ways you have been meeting your needs no longer hold in the same way.

Security: What once gave you security may feel restrictive.

Variety: What once brought variety may feel distracting or empty.

Self: What once helped you feel valued may feel performative.

Intimacy: What once gave you connection may feel surface-level.

Growth: What once felt like growth may feel forced.

Transcendence: What once gave you purpose may feel unclear.

The result is a full-system disruption. Nothing is broken. You are being invited to evolve.

When the Roots Begin to Speak

This experience often moves through your life root by root — sometimes all at once.

Health	You may feel it in your body first. Fatigue, restlessness, anxiety, or a loss of energy. Your system is asking for a different pace and a different kind of care.
Family	Old patterns surface. Beliefs about love, responsibility, success, or worth begin to feel outdated or limiting.
Relationships	Connections may feel distant or incomplete. There can be a pull toward deeper, more honest interaction.
Career	Work that once felt meaningful may begin to feel empty. Questions about direction, impact, and alignment come forward.
Friends	You may feel out of place in spaces where you once belonged. At the same time, there is a growing desire for more aligned connection.

It can feel disorienting, like your internal foundation is being reshaped. That is exactly what is happening. And it is meaningful.

The Identity Beneath It All

Part of the intensity comes from how deeply this touches your identity. Many of us build our sense of self around how we meet our needs across these roots. You may have become:

- The one who holds everything together
- The one who succeeds
- The one who shows up for everyone
- The one who adapts to belong
- The one who pushes through

These roles often created stability, connection, and success. And at some point, they may no longer reflect who you are becoming.

As these identities begin to loosen, it can feel like losing yourself. What is actually happening is a more honest connection to who you are now.

Moving Through, Not Around

There is no quick fix for this phase, and there is a way to move through it with awareness. It begins by listening to where your life is asking for attention.

Notice which root feels most activated. Notice what your body is communicating. Notice what your relationships are reflecting back. Pay attention to where your energy rises and where it shuts down.

There is no need to solve everything at once. Begin by noticing with honesty. This is where your power starts to return.

A New Way to See It

What if this moment is not the end of something working, but the quiet unraveling of something that was never fully true?

What if the discomfort is pointing you back to yourself?

This is not about finding answers right now. It is about building awareness — and letting that awareness guide what comes next. Move through these steps slowly. Come back to them as things shift.

1   **Identify Your Most Activated Root**
Which root feels most unstable, heavy, or out of alignment right now? Trust your first instinct.

Circle or write the root that feels most activated:

Health	Family	Relationships	Career	Friends

What feels off or out of alignment in this area of my life?

2   **Explore Your Emotional Needs**
For the root you selected, reflect on each need. Where does it feel most disrupted right now?

Security: Where do I feel uncertain or unstable?

Variety: Where do I feel stuck, bored, or overwhelmed?

Self: Where am I seeking validation or losing connection with myself?

Intimacy: Where do I feel disconnected or unable to be fully seen?

Growth: Where do I feel stagnant or pressured?

Transcendence: Where do I feel a lack of meaning or purpose?

Which needs feel most unmet right now? Write freely:

3 Look at Your Current Strategies

How have you been trying to meet these needs? Be honest, not harsh. Awareness is the goal.

Common patterns include: overworking to feel secure or valued, avoiding conflict to maintain connection, staying busy to avoid discomfort, or seeking external validation. What are yours?

How have I been trying to meet these needs up until now?

4 Notice What Is No Longer Working

This is where awareness deepens. Naming what is not working is not failure — it is the beginning of change.

Which of these strategies no longer feel aligned or effective?

<table>
<tr><td>**5**</td><td>

Reimagine Alignment

Let this be exploratory, not perfect. You are not solving the problem — you are opening to what is possible.
</td></tr>
</table>

What would it look like to meet these needs in a more honest or supportive way?

<table>
<tr><td>**6**</td><td>

One Aligned Step Forward

One small, grounded action. Not a plan. Not a solution. Just one thing that feels true right now.
</td></tr>
</table>

It could be a conversation. A boundary. A moment of rest. A new direction to explore. A permission you give yourself.

One step I can take this week to support myself is:

Closing Reflection

This is not about fixing everything at once. It is about beginning to understand what your life is asking for, and allowing that awareness to unfold in its own time.

The dark night of the soul marks a shift in your story. A moment where you start living with greater consciousness.

In the Root-to-Rise journey, this is part of the path. The moment you begin to question what no longer feels aligned is the moment your rise has already begun.

"You are not falling apart. You are falling open."

BONUS CHAPTER 3: THE LARGER LANDSCAPE

How the Root-to-Rise Framework Connects to the Wisdom You May Already Know

If you have spent any time exploring personal growth, therapy, philosophy, or spiritual practice, you have likely come across other frameworks along the way. Maslow. Jung. CBT. Stoicism. Yoga. Maybe some of them have shaped the way you see yourself and your life.

This chapter is for you.

Root-to-Rise was never designed to compete with the wisdom that already exists. It was designed to hold it. Think of it as a living ecosystem, a structure that can welcome and integrate many different approaches without losing its own center.

What follows is a guide to how Root-to-Rise connects to nine of the most widely known frameworks in personal growth, psychology, and philosophy. For each one, you will find a plain-language explanation of what it offers, how it maps to the Root-to-Rise Framework, and a reflection prompt to help you explore where it is alive in your own life.

You do not need to master all of these. You just need to know which ones are calling you.

How to Use This Chapter

Move through each section slowly. Notice which frameworks feel familiar and which feel new. Pay attention to where something resonates. Resonance is information. At the end of the chapter, there is a final reflection to help you identify which path or paths you want to explore more deeply as you continue your rise.

Internal Family Systems (IFS)

Your Inner Ecosystem

What It Is	How It Connects to Root-to-Rise	Reflection
IFS, developed by Dr. Richard Schwartz, teaches that we are made up of many internal parts — each with its own perspective, feelings, and protective role. At our center is the Self: calm, curious, and compassionate. The goal is not to eliminate parts but to build a relationship with them so that the Self can lead.	IFS is the inner map. Root-to-Rise is the outer structure. Where IFS helps you understand what is happening inside — which part is activated, what need it is trying to meet, how to respond with compassion — Root-to-Rise gives that inner experience a life context. Which root is this part showing up in? Which human need is it trying to protect? Together, they offer a complete picture: inner world and outer life, both held with awareness. For a deeper exploration, see Bonus Chapter One.	Which part of you has been most present during this workbook journey? What has it been protecting you from, and what might it be ready to release now that you have done this work?

Go Deeper

Think back to a moment during this workbook when you felt resistance, fear, or the urge to skip a section. Which part was that? What was it trying to protect? What would you say to it now?

Maslow's Hierarchy of Needs

The Universal Scaffolding

What It Is	How It Connects to Root-to-Rise	Reflection
Abraham Maslow proposed that human beings have a hierarchy of needs, from basic survival (food, shelter, safety) up through belonging, esteem, and finally self-actualization — the fullest expression of who we are. Most people know it as the pyramid.	Maslow gives us the universal scaffolding — the ladder every human must climb. Root-to-Rise is your full life ecosystem. Where Maslow shows what all humans need in sequence, Root-to-Rise asks: in your specific life, across your specific roots, how are those needs being met right now? The six human needs in Root-to-Rise go further by naming the emotional drivers behind each level — and by treating them as operating simultaneously, not in strict sequence.	Where in Maslow's hierarchy are you currently living? Are your safety needs solid? Or are you trying to self-actualize while a root beneath you is unstable?

Go Deeper

Think about your five life roots right now. Which roots feel most foundational and secure? Which ones are you trying to grow from before they are truly ready to hold you?

Jungian Psychology and Shadow Work

Below the Floorboards

What It Is	How It Connects to Root-to-Rise	Reflection
Carl Jung believed that the parts of ourselves we repress, deny, or disown — our shadow — do not disappear. They go underground and shape our behavior from below. Shadow work is the practice of bringing those hidden parts into conscious awareness so they lose their unconscious power over us.	Jung works below the floorboards. Root-to-Rise organizes the visible life structure above them. The Clearing phase of Root-to-Rise — where you examine fears, limiting beliefs, and hidden emotional traps — is where these two approaches most naturally meet. Your shadow often lives in the roots you avoid examining. Jungian work can make that examination deeper and more honest.	Which life root do you most resist looking at? What might be hiding there that you have not yet been willing to see?

Go Deeper

Think about a recurring pattern in your life, something that keeps showing up no matter how hard you try to change it. What hidden belief or disowned part might be driving it? What would it mean to bring it into the light?

Cognitive Behavioral Therapy (CBT)

Rewriting the Script

What It Is	How It Connects to Root-to-Rise	Reflection
CBT is one of the most researched approaches in psychology. Its core insight is simple: our thoughts shape our feelings, which shape our behavior. By identifying and challenging distorted or unhelpful thoughts, we can shift our emotional experience and change our patterns.	Root-to-Rise's Clearing phase — particularly Rewriting the Script and Hidden Emotional Traps — draws directly on CBT principles. Where CBT focuses on individual thought patterns, Root-to-Rise places those patterns in the context of your full life ecosystem, asking: which root is this thought living in? Which unmet need is it serving? CBT gives you the tool. Root-to-Rise gives you the map.	What is a story you keep telling yourself about one of your life roots — career, relationships, health — that may not actually be true? What would change if you challenged it?

Go Deeper

Write down a belief you hold about yourself that keeps you from fully nourishing one of your roots. Then write the opposite. Which one feels more true — and why?

Positive Psychology and PERMA

The Mirror and the Blueprint

What It Is	How It Connects to Root-to-Rise	Reflection
Positive Psychology, developed by Martin Seligman, focuses on what makes life worth living rather than what goes wrong. The PERMA model identifies five elements of wellbeing: Positive emotions, Engagement, Relationships, Meaning, and Achievement.	PERMA is a psychological mirror — it shows you where flourishing is present or absent. Root-to-Rise is a lived blueprint — it gives you the structure to build flourishing into your actual life. Where PERMA measures wellbeing, Root-to-Rise builds it. The five life roots add dimensions PERMA does not fully address: physical health, career logistics, family dynamics, and financial stability. Together, they create a more complete picture.	Which element of PERMA — positive emotion, engagement, relationships, meaning, or achievement — feels most alive in your life right now? Which feels most depleted?

Go Deeper

Look at your five life roots alongside PERMA. Where do they overlap? Where does one framework illuminate something the other misses? What does that tell you about where to focus your energy?

Stoicism

The Spartan Dojo vs. The Nourishing Greenhouse

What It Is	How It Connects to Root-to-Rise	Reflection
Stoicism is one of the oldest and most enduring philosophical traditions in the world. Its core practice is distinguishing between what is within our control and what is not, and focusing all of our energy on the former. It teaches resilience, clarity, and emotional regulation through discipline and reason.	Stoicism is a Spartan Dojo, built for discipline focused on constraint and fortitude. Root-to-Rise is a Nourishing Greenhouse built for growth, focused on meeting essential emotional needs. The two are not opposites. The Resilience phase of Root-to-Rise — particularly navigating the storms of life — reflects deeply Stoic principles. Where Stoicism teaches you to endure, Root-to-Rise also asks: what do you need to truly thrive, not just survive?	Where in your life are you practicing Stoic discipline, focusing only on what you can control? And where might you benefit from more nourishment rather than more endurance?

Go Deeper

Think about a challenge you are currently facing. Write two responses: the Stoic response (what can I control here?) and the Root-to-Rise response (what do I need to nourish myself through this?). Where do they meet?

Attachment Theory

The Roots of How We Love

What It Is	How It Connects to Root-to-Rise	Reflection
Attachment Theory, developed by John Bowlby and expanded by researchers like Mary Ainsworth, explores how our earliest bonds shape the way we relate to others throughout our lives. The four main attachment styles — secure, anxious, avoidant, and disorganized — influence how we experience intimacy, conflict, and connection.	Attachment Theory lives most directly in the Relationships and Family roots of the Root-to-Rise Framework. Your attachment style is one of the most powerful determinants of how your Intimacy need gets met, or goes unmet. Understanding your attachment patterns can illuminate why certain relationship dynamics keep repeating, and which root-level shifts might help you create more secure connection.	Do you know your attachment style? How does it show up in your relationships and family roots? What would more secure attachment feel like in your life?

Go Deeper

Think about your closest relationships. What patterns do you notice in how you give and receive connection? What does this tell you about your Intimacy need and your Relationships root?

Somatic Awareness

The Body as Root

What It Is	How It Connects to Root-to-Rise	Reflection
Somatic approaches to healing recognize that the body holds what the mind often cannot fully access or articulate. Trauma, stress, unmet needs, and emotional patterns live in the nervous system and the body's tissues, not just in our thoughts. Somatic practices include body scanning, breathwork, movement, and nervous system regulation.	In Root-to-Rise, the Health root is the foundation of everything, and the body is its most direct expression. The Resilience phase introduces the Triad of Physiology, Focus, and Meaning, which recognizes that your physical state directly shapes your emotional experience. Somatic awareness is the practice that brings the Health root alive. It is also how many people first detect a Dark Night of the Soul — through the body, before the mind has words for it.	Where do you feel your most activated life root in your body right now? What is your body trying to tell you that your mind has not yet caught up to?

Go Deeper

Take a slow breath and do a quick body scan from head to feet. Where do you notice tension, heaviness, or contraction? Where do you feel open or at ease? What root does each sensation live in?

Yoga Philosophy

The Ancient Ecosystem

What It Is	How It Connects to Root-to-Rise	Reflection
Yoga is far more than physical postures. As a philosophical tradition rooted in ancient Indian texts, yoga offers a complete framework for living — including ethical principles (the yamas and niyamas), an understanding of the self and consciousness, practices for mental clarity and emotional regulation, and a path toward liberation or integration. At its heart, yoga teaches that suffering comes from disconnection and that freedom comes from alignment — with the self, with others, and with something larger.	Yoga philosophy is perhaps the most naturally aligned of all the frameworks with Root-to-Rise because both treat life as a living system that requires tending, not forcing. The Taproot in Root-to-Rise — the question of what feeds your soul deeply — speaks directly to yoga's inquiry into dharma, or purpose. The Rise phase, with its emphasis on authenticity, legacy, and living your truth, reflects the yogic path toward integration. The ecological metaphor itself carries the spirit of yoga's understanding of interconnection.	What does your yoga or spiritual practice, formal or informal, bring to your Root-to-Rise journey? Where does it nourish your roots? Where might it deepen your rise?

Go Deeper

Yoga asks: what is your dharma — your unique purpose and path? How does your answer connect to your Taproot question: What feeds your soul deeply? Write whatever comes first, without editing it.

Your Larger Landscape

You have just moved through nine of the most powerful frameworks in human growth and wisdom. Some will have felt deeply familiar. Others may have opened a door you did not know was there. All of them are pointing in the same direction: toward a life that is more conscious, more aligned, and more fully yours.

Root-to-Rise is the ecosystem that holds all of this. It is your map. The frameworks above are trails you can explore from within it.

Final Reflection: Which Path Is Calling You?

Which one or two frameworks in this chapter resonated most strongly with you?

What is it about that framework that speaks to where you are right now in your life?

Which life root does that framework most directly address for you?

What is one concrete step you could take to explore it more deeply?

A Note to Close

The greatest teachers — whether ancient philosophers, modern psychologists, or the quiet wisdom of a life honestly lived — are all pointing at the same thing.

Know yourself. Tend your life. Live with intention.

Root-to-Rise is your home base. Everything else is an invitation to go deeper.

★ ★ ★

CONGRATULATIONS

You did something extraordinary.

Most people carry their dreams quietly and never go here.

You went inward.

You got honest.

You chose yourself.

★ ★ ★

This workbook asked a lot of you. It asked you to look honestly at your roots, to name the patterns that have held you back, to sit with grief and resistance and fear, and keep going anyway. That is not small. That is the work most people avoid their entire lives.

Every reflection you completed, every aha moment you captured, every truth you wrote down and had the courage to look at. All of it represents a real investment in your life. Not someday. Now.

WHAT YOU HAVE BUILT

- A deeper understanding of your Life Root System — and what truly nourishes you
- Awareness of the six human needs quietly driving your choices
- Tools to navigate your emotions instead of being ruled by them
- The courage to begin clearing what's been holding you back
- Resilience practices to steady you through life's hardest seasons
- A clearer, more honest relationship with your authentic self
- A vision for the balanced, purposeful life you are building
- Your Root-to-Rise Map — a living blueprint for everything ahead

---

Your Root-to-Rise Map is not a finished product; it's a living document. Return to it in moments of uncertainty. Update it as you grow, and easily create a revised version in the diagnostic tools as directed on glowliving.com. Let it remind you of who you are and what you're rising toward, especially when life gets hard and the path feels unclear.

The world doesn't need a perfect version of you. It needs the real, fully alive version of you. And you just spent all these pages becoming more of that person.

"You are not the same person who opened this workbook. And that's the whole point."

ABOUT THE AUTHOR

Chandra Lynn, MBA

Certified Transformation Coach | Strategic Consultant

Chandra Lynn is a certified transformation coach, creator of the Root-to-Rise System for Loving Life, and the author of the Amazon #1 bestselling book *Root-to-Rise: How to Love Life*.

She is the founder of Glow Living, a personal growth platform dedicated to helping people love life through emotional awareness and intentional living, and CEO of Glow Marketing LLC, where she has spent 25+ years leading marketing for some of the world's most recognized brands and artists.

Chandra's work bridges business strategy and emotional transformation, blending human needs psychology, coaching methodologies, yoga philosophy, and practical life strategy. Her approach is grounded in the belief that transformation happens when people understand why they do what they do, especially the emotional needs behind their decisions.

She speaks on emotional needs psychology, life pivots, authenticity, and what it truly means to build a life you love. Her work has been endorsed by Deepak Chopra and recognized by Kirkus Reviews, Readers' Choice and many others.

Connect with Chandra

Website: chandralynn.com
Instagram/Facebook: @GlowChandra
Linkedin: https://www.linkedin.com/in/chandralynn

CONTINUE YOUR JOURNEY

This workbook is one part of a larger ecosystem designed to support your rise. Here are some of what is available to you now. Stay tuned for new offerings.

The Root-to-Rise System for Loving Life

Deepen your personal development journey with main book *Root-to-Rise: How to Love Life*, this companion workbook, journals, card decks, training and diagnostic tools, and more.

Hidden Forces Quiz

Discover which of the six emotional needs is most driving your life right now.

Root-to-Rise Integration Circle

A community-based coaching program on The Life Lounge app to apply the framework with guidance, accountability, and connection.

Online Courses & Coaching

Self-paced courses and 1:1 coaching programs to go deeper into the Root-to-Rise system at your own pace.

Root-to-Rise Compass

Assess the health of your roots through 35 short ratings. Return monthly and watch your scores rise over time.

Root-to-Rise 24/7 Coach

Your personal coaching companion, available anytime. Ask questions, get guidance, and go deeper on any part of the framework — whenever you need free support.

STAY CONNECTED

- Visit ChandraLynn.com and GlowLiving.com and sign up for free updates, bonus resources, meditations, and journal pages
- Please leave a review on Amazon, Goodreads, and any other places you'd like to add support and help those in need find Root-to-Rise
- Explore your free Root-to-Rise AI Tools at glowliving.com — including the Hidden Forces Quiz, Root-to-Rise Compass, digital Map, and your Root-to-Rise 24/7 Coach
- Share your rise on social media: #RootToRiseBook • @GlowLiving • @GlowChandra
- Gift a copy. Become a book benefactor. Start a book circle. Rise together.

"I root in truth and rise in alignment. Rise, always."

— Chandra Lynn